21世纪英语专业系列教材

INTERCULTURAL COMMUNICATION: THEORY AND PRACTICE

跨文化交际教程

（第二版）

刘凤霞　编著
〔澳〕Carol Eames 审校

图书在版编目(CIP)数据

跨文化交际教程/刘凤霞编著.—2版.—北京:北京大学出版社,2009.3
(21世纪英语专业系列教材)
ISBN 978-7-301-08588-2

Ⅰ.跨… Ⅱ.刘… Ⅲ.交化交流-世界 Ⅳ.G115

书　　　名:	跨文化交际教程(第二版)
著作责任者:	刘凤霞　编著
责 任 编 辑:	李　颖
标 准 书 号:	ISBN 978-7-301-08588-2/H·1396
出 版 发 行:	北京大学出版社
地　　　址:	北京市海淀区成府路205号　100871
网　　　址:	http://www.pup.cn
电　　　话:	邮购部 62752015　发行部 62750672　编辑部 62767315
	出版部 62754962
电 子 邮 箱:	zbing@pup.pku.edu.cn
印　刷　者:	三河市博文印刷有限公司
经　销　者:	新华书店
	890毫米×1240毫米　A5　7.75印张　217千字
	2005年3月第1版　2009年3月第2版
	2022年12月第13次印刷(总第18次印刷)
定　　　价:	27.00元

未经许可,不得以任何方式复制或抄袭本书之部分或全部内容。
版权所有,侵权必究　举报电话:010-62752024
　　　　　　　　　　电子邮箱:fd@pup.pku.edu.cn

本书为教育部"新世纪高等教育教学改革工程"立项项目

《21世纪英语专业系列教材》编写委员会

（以姓氏笔画排序）

王守仁　王克非　申　丹
刘意青　李　力　胡壮麟
桂诗春　梅德明　程朝翔

总　　序

北京大学出版社自 2005 年以来已出版《语言与应用语言学知识系列读本》多种，为了配合第十一个五年计划，现又策划陆续出版《21 世纪英语专业系列教材》。这个重大举措势必受到英语专业广大教师和学生的欢迎。

作为英语教师，最让人揪心的莫过于听人说英语不是一个专业，只是一个工具。说这些话的领导和教师的用心是好的，为英语专业的毕业生将来找工作着想，因此要为英语专业的学生多多开设诸如新闻、法律、国际商务、经济、旅游等其他专业的课程。但事与愿违，英语专业的教师们很快发现，学生投入英语学习的时间少了，掌握英语专业课程知识甚微，即使对四个技能的掌握也并不比大学英语学生高明多少，而那个所谓的第二专业在有关专家的眼中只是学到些皮毛而已。

英语专业的路在何方？有没有其他路可走？这是需要我们英语专业教师思索的问题。中央领导关于创新是一个民族的灵魂和要培养创新人才等的指示精神，让我们在层层迷雾中找到了航向。显然，培养学生具有自主学习能力和能进行创造性思维是我们更为重要的战略目标，使英语专业的人才更能适应 21 世纪的需要，迎接 21 世纪的挑战。

如今，北京大学出版社外语部的领导和编辑同志们，也从教材出版的视角探索英语专业的教材问题，从而为贯彻英语专业教学大纲做些有益的工作，为教师们开设大纲中所规定的必修、选修课程提供各种教材。《21 世纪英语专业系列教材》是普通高等教育"十一五"国家级规划教材和国家"十一五"重点出版规划项目《面向新世纪的立体化网络化英语学科建设丛书》的重要组成部分。这套系列教材要体现新世纪英语教学的自主化、协作化、模块化和超文本化，结合外语教材的具体情况,既要解决语言、教学内容、教学方法和教育技术的时代化,也要坚持弘扬以爱国主义为核心的民族精神。因此,今天北京大学出版社在大力提倡专业英语教学改革的基础上,编辑出版各种英语专业技能、英语专业知识和相关专业知识课程的教材,以培养具有创新性思维的和具有实际工作能力的学生,充分体现了时代精神。

北京大学出版社的远见卓识,也反映了英语专业广大师生盼望已久的心愿。由北京大学等全国几十所院校具体组织力量,积极编写相关教材。这就是说,这套教材是由一些高等院校有水平有经验的第一线教师们制定编写大纲,反复讨论,特别是考虑到在不同层次、不同背景学校之间取得平衡,避免了先前的教材或偏难或偏易的弊病。与此同时,一批知名专家教授参与策划和教材审定工作,保证了教材质量。

当然,这套系列教材出版只是初步实现了出版社和编者们的预期目标。为了获得更大效果,希望使用本系列教材的教师和同学不吝指教,及时将意见反馈给我们,使教材更加完善。

航道已经开通,我们有决心乘风破浪,奋勇前进!

胡壮麟
北京大学蓝旗营

前　言

关于文化的界说，人们历来争论不休，莫衷一是。不论文化有多少不同的定义，有一点是很明确的，即文化的核心是人。"人既是文化的创造者，又是文化成果的享受者；既是文化的主体，又受着文化的制约；文化既是人的文化，人也是文化的人"（董广杰：2001）。人们的生活，无论是物质的还是精神的，始终是发生在特定的文化氛围中，而文化反过来又影响和形成人们的所思所想，所作所为。文化使得我们承继同一种文化遗产群体中的个体拥有共同的知识、信仰、价值观、生活方式、行为方式、思维方式、道德规范等；文化教给我们如何看待世界，如何判断美丑、正误，如何待人接物，如何表达情感。文化因素隐含在我们生活中的各个方面，小到准备什么样的早餐，大到如何处理国际间事务。可以说，文化无所不在，文化的辐射范围几乎无所不包。

人类学家将文化分为三个层次，即高级文化、大众文化、深层文化。高级文化包括哲学、文学、艺术、宗教等；大众文化则指人们在长期社会交往中约定俗成的风俗习惯、生活方式、行为模式等；深层文化指人们的价值观念、审美情趣、思维方式、时空观、道德观等。这三层文化紧密相联，深层文化是文化的核心和精华，是现实的根源。高级文化和大众文化均植根于深层文化，反过来，深层文化又通过人们的行为准则、生活习俗、艺术形式、文学作品等多种渠道和形式反映到大众文化和高级文化中。"生长于一种文化的人自然地继承了深层文化和大众文化。人们的思维与行为往往无形中被深层文化支配"（浦小君：1991）。例如，西方人的守时反映出其时间就是金钱的价值观；中国人常常以含蓄的方式表达不同看法，则反映出我们求同性的中庸和谐的价值取向。

作为文化的主要载体，语言与文化之间始终存在着不可分割的内在联系。譬如，在工业化社会里，其语言中反映技术的复杂性和专业性的词汇很多,而在以狩猎、种植为主的社会里,有关动、植物种类的词汇常常被人们所熟知。譬如,汉语中表示亲属关系的词名目繁多,且长幼有序,男女有别,血缘姻亲属性一目了然。这一特点源于汉民族封建宗法制度以及中国人重家庭、重亲属的传统文化。而英语中贫乏笼统的亲属称谓语则折射出英格兰民族平等看待亲属关系的文化特征。语言能够折射出一种文化对世界的感悟和认识,透过语言则能窥见一个民族绚丽多彩的文化。"当民族在人类历史上作为一种语言、居住区域、经济生活、心理状态上稳定的共同体出现时,语言就深深地打上了民族的烙印,成为民族文化最典型的表征。一个民族的文化心理结构深藏在民族语言之中,因而语言的结构具有民族文化的通约性"(张岱年、方克立:1994)。因此,语言不能脱离文化而存在,语言教学也不能忽视教授目的语文化。文化学习是培养学习者跨文化交际能力中不可或缺的内容。

有研究者指出,跨文化交际是一个综合系统,其中包括语言、文化、社会、心理等相互密切联系,并为交际提供适用的行为规范和准则的子系统。交际双方的语言行为和交流方式均受到双方共有的交际系统的影响和制约。如果中国的英语学习者用英语同英语本族人交流,他必须对英语民族在交际中所适用的规则和准则,以及隐含在这些规则和准则背后的社会、文化,尤其是民族文化心理、价值观等因素有尽可能多的了解,才能保证跨文化交际的顺利进行。不同的社会有不同的交流方式和规范,这些方式和规范无不受到文化的影响和制约。不同民族之所以有其特有的思维、感悟、信仰、行为,是因为他们所接受到的信息不同,以及这些信息中传递的文化不同。如我们从孩提时代就开始懂得该跟谁说话,说什么,怎么说,这些交际规则都来自日常生活中的耳濡目染。Hall指出,"文化即交际,交际即文化"两者之间联系如此紧密,以至于"很难区分哪个是原声(voice),哪个是回应(echo)"(转引自 Samovar et al:2000)。综上所述,在培养学习者跨文化交际能力的过程中,文化教学举足轻重。如果说自然语言是交际中的有声语言的话,那么文化就是交际中的无声语言,同样支配和制约着人们的交际活动。

传统意义上的文化教学是教授目的语国家的历史、地理、国家机构、文学艺术以及影响理解文学作品的背景知识。自20世纪四五十年代以来,随着社会科学,尤其是人类学和社会学的发展和影响,语言学、教学专家们开始认识到,了解和分析一个民族的居住环境、生活方式以及他们的思想、行为对于学习该民族的语言十分重要,并研究将这些内容纳入文化教学。

  本书试图从文化课中的文化教学入手,从大的文化框架内选择了一些反映目的语文化现象的主题进行讨论与对比,如家庭、教育、工作、体育、保健等,并选择编入了一些国内外在中西方文化对比研究领域中的相关成果,旨在通过对英语国家较为典型的主流文化现象进行描述、阐释、讨论以及与我们本国文化的对比,培养学生对目的语文化的兴趣和理解力,进而使他们主动观察、分析、对比、评价,并从深层文化探讨和研究中西方文化之间存在的差异,以有效提高学生的跨文化交际能力,为他们能够较为客观、系统、全面地认识英语国家的文化,宣传本国文化打下基础。

  本书每一单元主要内容分两个部分:阅读与讨论和课堂任务,所涉及的内容大多属探索性的。阅读材料用来提供有关背景知识,课堂教学很大程度上是在给学生留有思考、探讨空间、开放式的讨论中进行。主要课堂活动是学生在小组内讨论并完成相关任务,即用目的语对英语国家和本国特定的文化现象进行调查、描述、分析、讨论、辩论、演讲等。学生在对某个特定文化现象进行观察、调查、搜集资料、分析、发表见解的过程中,锻炼其获取知识、多角度观察事物、思考问题、学习进行科学研究的方法和能力。本书的附录对课文中的讨论题及课堂任务提供了部分参考。

  本书借鉴国外相关教材的编写方法,结合我国英语教学实际编写而成,适合于英语专业、大学英语教师、本科生和研究生,以及英语翻译、导游和英语爱好者。

  付永钢副教授增补了第12章,北京大学出版社的张冰主任和李颖编辑对本书的出版和修订给予了热情的支持,笔者一并向他们表示衷心的感谢。

  由于笔者水平有限,书中难免有疏漏和错误,诚请专家、同行和广大读者不吝指教。

Acknowledgements

We are indebted, mainly for the reading selections, to many sources. We have put forth the fullest effort to trace each and every source, and their origins and our acknowledgements are indicated within the book. However, a small number of copyright materials remain uncredited because the original copyright holders could not be located, or we were unable to establish communication with them. It may be the case that some unintentional omissions have occurred in the employment of some copyright materials. We are grateful to these authors and sources, and we apologize for not being able to extend our acknowledgements in detail. For any questions concerning copyrights and permissions, please contact

Copyrights Department
Peking University Press
Beijing, 100871
P. R. China
Telephone: +86 10 62752036
Fax: +86 10 62556201
Email: xiena@pup.pku.edu.cn

We are much obliged for any information concerned and will make necessary arrangements for the appropriate settlement of any possible copyright issue.

CONTENTS
目　录

前言 ·· (1)
Acknowledgements ··· (4)

Unit 1　Communication and Culture ·················· (3)
　　　　交际与文化

Unit 2　Language ·· (15)
　　　　语言

Unit 3　Non-Verbal Communication ··················· (29)
　　　　非语言交际

Unit 4　Family Values ·· (47)
　　　　家庭观

Unit 5　Education ·· (63)
　　　　教育

Unit 6　Work Values ·· (81)
　　　　工作观

Unit 7　Business Attitudes ······································ (99)
　　　　生意观

Unit 8　Leisure and Sports ···································· (115)
　　　　休闲与体育

Unit 9　Food and Healthcare …………………………… (133)
　　　　食品与保健

Unit 10　Interpersonal Relationships …………………… (153)
　　　　人际关系

Unit 11　Intercultural Awareness ………………………… (171)
　　　　跨文化交际意识

Unit 12　Intercultural Communication Competence ……… (187)
　　　　跨文化交际能力

Appendix　Additional Information for Some of the Discussion
　　　　Questions ………………………………………… (203)
　　　　部分参考答案

References ……………………………………………………… (231)

交际与文化

　　培养跨文化交际意识旨在通过对不同文化的客观比较和对比,使语言学习者领悟自身文化,理解别国文化,排除民族中心论,欣赏文化多元性,进而与操本族语言者有效交际。

　　文化和交际不可分割。人们所有交际活动都受其文化的支配和制约。我们用语言进行交际,而语言在很大程度上又受到文化的影响。因此,学习用一种新的语言与其本族人交际,就要掌握一种新的规范和新的价值体系。语言和文化与我们如此密不可分,以至于使我们将它们视为自然,习以为常,甚至常常用本民族的习惯与规范去审视其他民族的行为。本族人受其交际规范潜移默化的影响,耳濡目染,通常是自然习得。而对语言学习者来说,只有通过有意识地学习,才能获得别国文化的相应的知识。跨文化交际研究,致力于将某一民族人与人之间相互理解和交际的无意识知识明确化。学习者在阅读本章过程中将获得跨文化交际的一些必要知识。

Unit 1 ①

Communication and Culture

Studying a second language without learning the culture is like learning how to drive a car by studying a driver's manual and never getting behind a steering wheel. ②

Reading and Discussion

Cross-Cultural Awareness

Developing cross-cultural awareness usually goes along with learning a new language and being exposed to a new culture; such exposure reveals both cultural similarities and differences. And sometimes it is the similarities between cultures that surprise us as much as the differences. Once a little four-year-old American traveling in China was overheard exclaiming, "Look, Mommy, that little Chinese boy is eating ice cream, too."

Cross-cultural awareness is the ability to understand cultures—your own and others'—by means of objective, non-judgmental comparisons. It is an appreciation for, an understanding of, cultural pluralism—the ability to get rid of our ethnocentric tendencies and to accept another culture on its own terms. Many cross-cultural interactions go sour due to a lack of such an awareness.

We study a foreign language in order to communicate with people who have learned their native language not in a classroom, but in natural, everyday interactions with people and situations in their culture. They have learned the intentions behind words and phrases mostly without consciously thinking about them; it has been part of their culture and they have taken it for granted. We, however, as adults learning a second language, must make a conscious effort to examine the cultural context of the language we want to learn.

Discussion

1. Discuss the following questions in groups.
—What does the "exclamation" of the little American reflect?
—What does "ethnocentric tendencies" mean?
2. Comment on the following views.
—Studying a second language without learning the culture is like learning how to drive a car by studying a driver's manual and never getting behind a steering wheel.
— As adults learning a second language we must make a conscious effort to examine the cultural context of the language we want to learn.

Passage 2

Communication

It has been said that without a culture we cannot see, but with a culture we are forever blind. In other words, each of us is born into a culture that teaches us a number of shared meanings and expectations. We usually learn our own culture's ways of doing, speaking, and thinking so well that it becomes difficult to think, feel, speak, and act as people in other cultures do.

As the basic building blocks of communication, words communicate meaning, but as we have seen, the meanings of words are very much influenced by culture. Meaning is in the person, not in the word, and each person is the product of a particular culture that passed on shared and appropriate meanings. Thus, if we want to learn to communicate well in a foreign language, we must understand the culture that gives that language meaning. In other words, culture and communication are inseparably linked: you can't have one without the other. Culture gives meaning and provides the context for communication, and the ability to communicate allows us to act out our cultural values and to share our language and our culture.

But our own native language and culture are so much a part of us that we take them for granted. When we travel to another country, it's as if we carry, along with our passports, our own culturally designed lenses through which we view the new environment. Using our own culture as the standard by which to judge other cultures is called ethnocentrism, and although unintentional, our ethnocentric ways of thinking and acting often get in the way of our understanding other languages and cultures. The ability and willingness to change lenses when we look at a different culture is both the cure and the prevention for such cultural blindness. Studying a new language provides the opportunity to practice changing lenses when we also learn the context of the culture to which it belongs.

When linguists study a new language they often compare it to their own, and consequently they gain a better understanding of not only the new language but of their own language as well. Students who study a foreign language will also learn more about their own native tongue by comparing and contrasting the two languages. You can follow the same comparative method in learning more about culture—your own, as well as others'. Remember that each culture has developed a set of patterns that are right and appropriate for that culture. If people do things differently in another culture, they are not "wrong"—they are just different! Always thinking that "culturally different" means "culturally wrong" will only promote intercultural misunderstanding.

The clothes we wear, the way we decorate our homes, the car we drive, the way we address people, the jobs we choose, the mates we choose—all these things communicate different things to different people, and they may communicate more, or less, than we intend. It depends on how the receiver of the message sees, thinks and feels as much as on what the sender says, thinks, and feels. Communication is a very complex process, even among people from the same culture who speak the same language. The potential problems and the likelihood of miscommunication multiply when communication takes place between people from different cultures.

Intercultural communication occurs whenever a person from one culture does something that is given meaning by a person from another culture. Communicating across cultures is made difficult by each person's ethnocentric tendencies to perceive objects, events, and behavior through lenses designed in the person's own culture. But an honest desire to communicate with people from other cultures, coupled with an attempt to understand cultural differences, will go a long way in helping you become a successful intercultural communicator.

Communicating in a new culture means learning what to say

(words, phrases, meaning, structure), who to communicate with (the role and status of the person), who you are (how you perceive yourself), how you communicate the message (emotional components, nonverbal cues, intonation), why you communicate in a given situation (intentions, values, assumptions), when to communicate (time), and where you can or should communicate. This sounds like an impossible task—but remember, you learned to do all these things in your own native language and culture, mostly without thinking about them. The difference is that now as an adult learning a second language and culture, you must think about the process.

Discussion

1. In small groups interpret the following ideas with examples.

— Meaning is in the person, not in the word.

— Culture and communication are inseparable.

— We tend to take our own language and culture for granted.

— People everywhere tend to be ethnocentric and are often not aware of cultural differences.

— Studying a foreign language helps one understand one's own language.

— Thinking that "culturally different" means "culturally wrong" will promote intercultural misunderstanding.

— Much of what we communicate is nonverbal.

2. The last paragraph of Passage 2 describes the complicated process of communication in a new culture. The American sociolinguist D. Hymes pointed out that people with communicative competence should know when, where and what to speak to whom and how.

In small groups, draw some implications from the research on communication and culture for second/foreign language learning (e. g. What should be included in second/foreign language teaching and learning besides the structure, grammar, words... of a language?)

3. Work individually. In retrospect, have you ever come across any frustrations or misunderstandings in cross-cultural communication caused by a lack of the knowledge of the target culture? If you have, share them with your group and give your possible explanations to those happenings. How might a course in cross-cultural awareness have helped you avoid your dilemma?

4. A wife has said to her husband: *"Yes, George. I know you can talk, but I want you to communicate."* What does she mean? What is the difference in meaning between "talk" and "communicate"? What does the word "communicate" connote that "talk" doesn't?

What is Culture?

By "culture" anthropology means the total life way of a people, the social legacy the individual acquires from his group. Or culture can be regarded as that part of the environment that is the creation of man.

This technical term has a wider meaning than the "culture" of history and literature. A humble cooking pot is as much a cultural product as is a Beethoven sonata. In ordinary speech a man of culture is a man who can speak languages other than his own, who is familiar with history, literature, philosophy, or the fine arts. In

Unit 1

some cliques that definition is still narrower. The cultured person is one who can talk about James Joyce[3], Scarlatti[4], and Picasso[5]. To the anthropologist, however, to be human is to be cultured. There is culture in general, and then there are the specific cultures such as Russian, American, British, Hottentot[6], Inca[7]. The general abstract notion serves to remind us that we cannot explain acts solely in terms of the biological properties of the people concerned, their individual past experience, and the immediate situation. The past experience of other men in the form of culture enters into almost every event. Each specific culture constitutes a kind of blueprint for all of life's activities.

Culture regulates our lives at every turn. From the moment we are born until we die there is, whether we are conscious of it or not, constant pressure upon us to follow certain types of behavior that other men have created for us. Some paths we follow willingly, others we follow because we know no other way, still others we deviate from or go back to most unwillingly. Mothers of small children know how unnaturally most of this comes to us—how little regard we have, until we are "culturalized,"[8] for the "proper" place, time, and manner for certain acts such as eating, excreting, sleeping, getting dirty, and making loud noises. But by more or less adhering to a system of related designs for carrying out all the acts of living, a group of men and women feel themselves linked together by a powerful chain of sentiments. Ruth Benedict[9] gave an almost complete definition of the concept when she said, "Culture is that which binds men together."

Every group's way of life, then, is a structure—not a haphazard collection of all the different physically possible and functionally effective patterns of belief and action. A culture is an interdependent system based upon linked premises and categories whose influence is greater, rather than less, because they are seldom put in words. Some degree of internal coherence which is felt rather than rationally constructed seems to be demanded by most of the participants in any culture. As Whitehead has remarked, "Human life is driven forward by its dim apprehension of notions too general for its existing language."

In sum, the distinctive way of life that is handed down as the social heritage of a people does more than supply a set of skills for making a living and a set of blueprints for human relations. Each different way of life makes its own assumptions about the ends and purposes of human existence, about what human beings have a right to expect from each other and the gods, about what constitutes fulfillment or frustration. Some of these assumptions are made explicit in the lore of the folk; others are tacit premises which the observer must infer by finding consistent trends in word and deed.

Discussion

1. Culture is classified into two large categories: one is in its narrow sense (Culture) and the other is in its broad, anthropological sense (culture). Discuss their meanings in pairs.

2. In Passage 3 the author discusses a wide range of characteristics of culture. How do you understand them? In small groups discuss your interpretation of these characteristics with examples.

— To be human is to be cultured.

— Each specific culture constitutes a kind of blueprint for all of life's activities.

— Culture regulates our lives at every turn.

— Culture is that which binds men together.

— Human life is driven forward by its dim apprehension of

notions too general for its existing language.

Notes

① Passages 1 and 2 are extracted from Irving, K. J., 1986, *Communication in Context*: *Intercultural Communication Skills for ESL Students*, New Jersey: Prentice-Hall, p. 31 and pp. 2—6.
Passage 3 is extracted from Kluckhohn, C., *Mirror for Man*: *The Relation of Anthropology to Modern Life*, in 胡文仲, 1990, *Selected Readings in Intercultural Communication*, 湖南教育出版社, pp. 35—42.
② Irving, K. J. 1986. *Communication in Context*: *Intercultural Communication Skills for ESL Students*. New Jersey: Prentice-Hall.
③ James Joyce: 詹姆斯·乔伊斯(1882—1941), 爱尔兰作家。
④ Scarlatti: 亚历山德罗·斯卡拉蒂(1660—1725), 意大利歌剧作曲家。
⑤ Picasso: 毕加索(1881—1973), 西班牙著名画家。
⑥ Hottentot: (西南非洲的)霍敦督族。
⑦ Inca: 印加人(南美印第安人的一个部落)。
⑧ culturalized: 受文化熏陶的。
⑨ Ruth Benedict (1887—1948): 美国著名人类学家。

语　　言

　　语言和文化相互依存,不可分割。语言既是文化的组成部分,又是文化的传播媒介。这种复杂的关系反映在语言结构的各个层面,如音位、词法、句法、词汇、语义和语言运用的各个方面。譬如,在对两种语言的翻译过程中,常常出现词汇、习语、语法、经验、概念等不对等问题。要使译文的接受者对译文的理解和欣赏与其原文的接受者对原文的理解和欣赏相一致,译者就要对两种相关语言所涉及的地理、历史、宗教、政治、传统、文化等方面有较深入的了解,并对它们进行对比、分析和研究。本章收集了一些中英两种语言对比研究的实例,设计了课堂讨论,旨在引发学习者在这方面的意识和思考,以提高他们的跨文化交际能力。

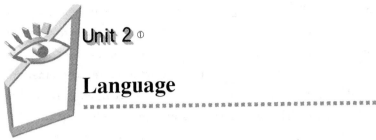

Unit 2[1]

Language

No one when he uses a word has in mind exactly the same thing that another has, and the difference, however tiny, sends its tremors throughout language.[2]

Reading and Discussion

Language

The fact that linguistic symbols are nearly all arbitrary—that is, they are conventions by which certain sounds are attached to certain objects and events—emphasizes the social aspects of language. In this sense, language is a part of culture.

Every language has a structure: an internal logic and a particular relationship between its parts. Structural linguistics shows that the structure of any language consists of four subsystems: phonology (a system of sounds), morphology (a system for creating words from sounds), syntax (a series of rules for combining words into meaningful sentences), and semantics (a system that relates words to meaning).

Phonology[3]. All languages use only a limited number of

sounds out of the vast range of sounds that can be made by the human vocal apparatus. Sounds used in one language may be absent in other languages. English, for example, does not use many of the tonal sounds of Chinese. Furthermore, combinations of sounds are used in different ways in different languages. For example, an English speaker can easily pronounce the ng sound in thing at the end of an utterance but not at the beginning; however, this sound is used in the initial position in Bambara, a language of Africa.

Most languages use only about thirty phonemes in their structure. By an unconscious process, the native speaker of a language not only learns to make the sounds used in the language but also to differentiate between sounds that are significant (phonemes) and those that are not. The ordinary person does not consciously think about the phonemic pattern of his or her language. Only when trying to learn another language or hearing someone with a thick foreign accent speak one's own language does one become aware of the variation in sounds and phonemes.

Morphology④. A morpheme is the small unit of a language that has a meaning. In English, -s, as in *dogs*, means "plural"; *un-* means "negative" as in *undo*; -er means "one who does," as in teacher. Because -s, *un-*, and -er are not used by themselves but only in association with another unit of meaning, they are called bound morphemes. A morpheme such as *giraffe* is called a free morpheme because it can stand alone. A word is the smallest part of a sentence that can be said alone and still retain its meaning. Some words consist of only one morpheme. *Giraffe* is an example of a single-morpheme word. *Teacher* has two morphemes, teach and -er.

Languages differ in the extent to which their words tend to contain only one, several, or many morphemes. In Chinese, most words have only one morpheme. English, like Chinese, has many single-morpheme words but also has many words that contain more than one morpheme. English also has words with three, four, or even more morphemes: The word undesirables has four morphemes: un-, desire, -able, and -s.

Syntax[5]. Syntax is the arrangement of words to form phrases and sentences. Languages differ in their syntactic structures. In English, word order is important because it conveys meaning. The syntax of the English language gives a different meaning to these two sentences: "The dog bit the man" and "The man bit the dog." In Latin, however, the subject and object of a sentence are indicated by word endings rather than word order.

Linguists agree that the grammatical categories of one language cannot be used to describe another language. Languages differ in the numbers and kinds of grammatical categories they have and how these categories are indicated. Thus, the information that in English would be expressed as "The dog bit the man" would be "Dog bite man" in Chinese. In Chinese, the tense of the verb need not be indicated, as it must be in English, although it can be brought in by using a time word such as *now* or *yesterday*.

The lexicon[6]. A lexicon is the total stock of words in a language. The relationship between culture and language is clearly seen in a lexicon. In industrial societies, the lexicon contains many words reflecting technological complexity and specialization. In technologically simpler societies, the lexicon has few such words. The lexicon of any culture reflects what is most important in that culture. For example, whereas the average American can name only about fifty to one hundred species of plants, members of societies based on hunting and gathering or on gardening can typically name five hundred to one thousand species of plants. In English, for example, the term *brother-in-law* can include my sister's husband, my husband's brother, and the husbands of all my husband's sisters. In Chinese, however, there are separate terms for my sister's husband, my husband's elder brother, my husband's younger brother, and my husband's sisters' husbands. Kinship vocabulary is a good clue to the nature of the most significant family relations in a culture. The single term brother-in-law in English reflects the similarity of a woman's behavior toward all the men in those different kinship statuses. The variety of words in Chinese reflects the fact that each of these categories of people is treated differently.

We have just seen how language reflects cultural emphases and the way in which cultures divide up their physical and social environment. But language does more than just reflect culture: It is the way in which the individual is introduced to the order of the physical and social environment. Therefore, language would seem to have a major impact on the way an individual perceives and conceptualizes the world.

Discussion

1. Passage 1 provides some examples of differences in Chinese and English languages. Using more examples, compare and contrast the two languages in phonology, morphology, syntax and the lexicon.

2. What makes the Chinese language special or unique?

3. What features of the Chinese language make it easier or more difficult for you to learn English?

Passage 2

Translation Problems

Even when cultures speak the same language—as the United States and Great Britain—there can be vocabulary differences. When cultures speak diverse languages, translation is critical—but always imperfect. Sechrest, Fay, and Zaidi (1972) have identified five translation problems that can become barriers to intercultural communication:

Vocabulary equivalence. First is the lack of vocabulary equivalence. Consider the discussion of the Sapir-Whorf[①] hypothesis. The Arctic people have many different words to refer to snow. Were you to translate on a word-for-word basis, you would translate all those different words into the one English word "snow." Much of the meaning of their more specific and more descriptive words—for example, qualities of slushiness or hardness or newness—would be lost. As another example, imagine having to translate all shades of pink, burgundy, orange-red, and so on into one word "red." As you might imagine, such a limitation would be frustrating to you if you were accustomed to using more descriptive words.

Idiomatic equivalence. The second barrier to successful translation is the problem of idiomatic equivalence. The English language is particularly replete with idioms. Take the simple example of "the old man kicked the bucket." Native speakers know that this idiom means the old man died. If the sentence is translated word for word, the meaning conveyed would be exactly that the old man kicked the bucket—quite different from the intended meaning.

Grammatical-syntactical equivalence. Third is the problem of grammatical-syntactical equivalence. This simply means that languages do not necessarily have the same grammar. Often, you need to understand a language's grammar to understand the meaning of words. For example, words in English can be nouns or verbs or adjectives depending on their position in a sentence. In English you can say "plan a table" and "table a plan" or "book a place" and "place a book" or "lift a thumb" and "thumb a lift."

Experiential equivalence. Fourth is the problem of experiential equivalence. If an object or experience does not exist in your culture, it is difficult to translate words referring to that object or experience into that language when no words may exist for them. Think of objects or experiences that exist in your culture and not in another. "Department store" and "shopping mall" may be as difficult to translate into some languages as "wind surfing" is into others.

Conceptual equivalence. Finally, the problem of conceptual equivalence refers to abstract ideas that may not exist in the same fashion in diverse languages. For example, in the United States they have a unique meaning for the word "freedom." That meaning is not universally shared. Speakers of other languages may say they are free and be correct in their culture, but that freedom they refer to is not equivalent to what you experience as freedom. Post-Communist Russians readily embraced the words "democracy," "congress" and "president," but having just broken with the totalitarian tradition, many had trouble understanding the underlying concepts.

Discussion

In small groups, do the following activities and reflect on the translation problems discussed in Passage 2. Try to think of more examples under the headings.

1) Vocabulary equivalence. Give the English equivalents of the following Chinese: "杯子", "疼/痛", (足球、篮球、高尔夫球等) "场".

Give the Chinese translation of the following English phrases:

a heavy rain, a heavy responsibility, heavy food, a heavy heart, heavy music;

The man fell. The prices fell. Her hair fell to her waist. He fell in love. The city fell.

2) Experiential equivalence. Translate the following Chinese into English and vise versa.

"四合院", "雍和宫", "武术", "三八妇女红旗手";
"Zeus," "monarchy," "hippie."

3) Conceptual equivalence. In groups discuss what the following words and their Chinese translation mean to the majority of people in both Chinese and Western cultures. Then think of more words that have different connotation in Chinese or English translation.

liberalism/自由主义   intellectual/知识分子
individualism/个人主义   peasant/农民
bureaucracy/官僚   human rights/人权
privilege/特权   propaganda/宣传
loyalty/忠   work/工作
filiality/孝   leisure/休闲

Classroom Tasks

Samovar, et al, in their book *Communication between Cultures* (2000: 123), pointed out that although complete acceptance of the Sapir-Whorf hypothesis may be controversial, its application to culture and language is clear: language is a reflection of culture, and culture is a reflection of language. Culture influences language by way of symbols and rules as well as our perception of the universe. Equally important is the fact that meaning shifts from culture to culture. In small groups, discuss in what way the languages of English and Chinese reflect their cultures (or vice versa) while doing the following tasks.

Task 1

Contrast the following two groups of sayings in both English and Chinese cultures and discuss the idea that language is a reflection of culture (consider the history and geography in both cultures).

1) A smooth sea never makes a skillful mariner.

2) He who would search for pearls must dive below.

3) Living without an aim is like sailing without a compass.

4) To have another fish to fry.

5) The water that bears the boat is the same that swallows it up.

6) 前人种树,后人乘凉。

7) 斩草不除根,逢春必要生。

8) 种田不用问,深耕多上粪。

9) 生米煮成了熟饭。

10) 巧妇难为无米之炊。

Task 2

Contrast the following two groups of sayings in both English and Chinese cultures and discuss the idea that language is a reflection of culture (consider the religions adhered to in both cultures).

1) Man proposes, God disposes.

2) God helps those who help themselves.

3) Forbidden fruit is sweetest.

4) as poor as the church mouse

5) The devil dances in an empty pocket.

6) 借花献佛。

7) 跑了和尚跑不了庙。

8) 做一天和尚撞一天钟。

9) 平时不烧香,临时抱佛脚。

10) 泥菩萨过河,自身难保。

Task 3

What values do these proverbs express? Which of these proverbs do you think characterize Western behavior and philosophy?

1) A stitch in time saves nine.

2) Take care of today, and tomorrow will take care of itself.

3) Time is money.

4) Time and tide wait for no man.

5) Early to bed, early to rise, makes a man healthy, wealthy, and wise.

6) Do not put off until tomorrow what you can do today.

7) Kill two birds with one stone.

8) If at first you don't succeed, try, try again. God helps those who help themselves.

9) A rolling stone gathers no moss.

10) You can't tell a book by its cover.

11) Clothes make the man.

12) Good fences make good neighbors.

13) Strike while the iron is hot.

14) Actions speak louder than words.

15) The squeaky wheel gets the grease.

Task 4

Animals are used to indicate different associative meanings in different languages. In small group, study the following expressions or sayings involving animals in both English and Chinese and discuss their cultural implications respectively.

The snake:

1) He that has been bitten by a serpent is afraid of a rope.

2) a snake in the grass

3) to warm a snake in one's bosom

4) a snake in the bosom

5) the serpent in Eden

6) 杯弓蛇影

7) 强龙不压地头蛇

8) 蛇爬无声,奸计无影

9) 蛇蝎心肠

The dragon:

1) chase the dragon

2) 龙马精神

3) 龙飞凤舞

4) 龙凤呈祥

5) 龙腾虎跃

6) 龙的传人

7) 望子成龙

The dog:

1) a lucky dog

2) Love me, love my dog.

3) Every dog has his day.

4) Barking dogs do not bite.

5) to teach an old dog new tricks

6) Let sleeping dog lie.

7) a dog in the manger

8) go to the dogs

9) 狗头军师

10) 狗仗人势

11) 狗急跳墙
12) 狗苟蝇营
13) 狗嘴里吐不出象牙
14) 儿不嫌母丑,狗不嫌家贫
15) 好狗护三邻,好汉护三村

Task 5

It has been realized that basic color terms could arouse cross-cultural misunderstanding. Compare and discuss the cultural connotations of the following color terms in English and Chinese.

1) red carpet
2) red-letter day
3) a red battle
4) red hands
5) red-light district
6) 开门红
7) 红事
8) 红运
9) 红颜
10) white hands
11) a white lie
12) a white hope
13) white list
14) 白事
15) 白丁
16) 白费力气
17) 白眼
18) 白色恐怖
19) a yellow dog
20) 黄帝
21) 黄袍
22) 炎黄子孙

23）黄道吉日
24）黄河
25）黄土地

① Passage 1 is extracted from Warms, S. & Warms, R. C., 1998, *Cultural Anthropology* 6th ed, Washington: Wadsworth Publishing Company, pp. 63—70.
Passage 2 is extracted from Jandt, F. E., 1995, *International Communication: An Introduction*, California: Sage Publication Ltd., pp. 111—113.

② *Humanist Without Portfolio: An Anthology of the Writing of Wilhelm von Humboldt* (p. 235), translated by Marianne Cowan, 1963, Detroit: Wayne State University Press, cited from Jandt, F. E., ibid, p. 110.

③ phonology：音位学。

④ morphology：形态学。

⑤ syntax：句法。

⑥ lexicon：词汇。

⑦ The Sapir-Whorf hypothesis：萨丕尔-沃尔夫假说（包括语言决定论 linguistic determinism 和语言相关论 linguistic relativity），认为看待世界的方法由其本族语的结构所决定。

非语言交际

所有人类文化都使用非语言形式进行交际,如面部表情、身体姿态动作、目视行为、空间处理、时间取向等。美国人类学家霍尔(E. Hall)在大量观察本国人交际过程中空间使用情况的基础上将空间占据分成四种:亲密距离、个人距离、社会距离和公众距离。还有一些研究表明,距离与占位不仅与亲密程度有关,还与人的社会地位、谈话的场合分布(圆形、长形等)以及内容有关。在时间观念上,不同文化背景的人对时间持有不同的态度和取向。霍尔把时间观念分为"单一记时制"(monochronic time)和"多向记时制"(polychronic time)。前者将时间看作是一条线,某个规定的时间是这条线上的点,两点之间的空间则是一段时间,人们的活动严格按照时间进行;后者把时间看作是点,在同一时间可进行几项活动。在交际中有些非语言形式是有意识的,有些是无意识的。一种文化接受的非语言形式可能完全不被另一种文化接受,甚至传达相反的含义。而正是这些千差万别的"无声语言"常常引起交际双方间的相互误解,成为跨文化交际的障碍。本单元收集了一些对非语言行为有影响的研究,以及中国人在与英语本族人交际过程中发生的文化冲撞案例,以引发学习者的思考和讨论。

Unit 3 ①

Non-Verbal Communication

Nonverbal communication involves all those nonverbal stimuli in a communication setting that are generated by both the source and his or her use of the environment and that have potential message value for the source or receiver.

——Samovar, L. A. et al. ②

Reading and Discussion

Body Language

People in all cultures use nonverbal gestures to communicate. Some of these gestures are conscious; some are unconscious. What people say with their facial expressions, for example, is a powerful form of communication. What is acceptable in one culture may be completely unacceptable in another. One culture may determine that snapping fingers to call a waiter is appropriate; another may consider this gesture rude. We are often not aware of how gestures, facial expressions, eye contact, and the use of space affect communication, when we are not aware of their meaning within a culture. Just like cultural norms it would be impossible for anyone to learn all the possible nonverbal communication behavior meanings. While we expect language to be different, we are less likely to expect and recognize how the nonverbal symbols are different.

Many nonverbal expressions vary from culture to culture, and it is just those variations that make nonverbal misinterpretation a barrier. Judee Burgoon (1986) has identified two perspectives on nonverbal communication: She writes that much nonverbal communication does have consensually recognized meanings and consistent usage within a culture and as such forms a vocabulary of nonverbal symbols. She also contends that some nonverbal communications, even in the same culture, are so ambiguous that their interpretation is mediated by context. Comparing observations and interpretations of nonverbal symbols often will reveal their ambiguity.

The example is given of a United States technical instructor in Iran who complained that his students weren't paying any attention to him. The basis of the instructor's inference was that his Iranian students were passively sitting and staring at him instead of taking notes on the important points of his lecture. On the basis of his experience with students in the United States who expect lectures to supplement texts, he believed that note-taking is a nonverbal cue signaling interests and the lack of note-taking is a cue signaling boredom or distraction. He failed to learn that Iranian students expect lectures to correspond exactly to the text so that they perceive no need to take notes.

Discussion

Work in small groups and discuss the following tasks.

1. Support the following opinions taken from Passage 1 with

examples.

— Some of these gestures are conscious; some are unconscious.

— What people say with their facial expressions is a powerful form of communication.

— What is acceptable in one culture may be completely unacceptable in another.

— Some nonverbal communications are ambiguous even in the same culture.

2. What do you think caused the misunderstanding between the American technical instructor and his Iranian students?

3. Have you ever experienced non-verbal communication misunderstanding between different ethnic communities or age groups?

The Message in Distance and Location[*]

Professor Hall's③ particular concern is the misunderstandings that can develop because people from different cultures handle space in very different ways. For two unacquainted adult male North Americans, for example the comfortable distance to stand for conversation is about two feet apart. The South American likes to stand much closer, which creates problems when a South American and a North American meet face to face. The South American who moves in to what is to him a proper talking distance may be considered "pushy" by the North American; and the North

---

* In this passage the pronoun "we" refers to American people.

American may seem standoffish to the South American when he backs off to create a gap of the size that seems right to him. Hall once watched a conversation between a Latin and a North American that began at one end of a forty-foot hall and eventually wound up at the other end, the pair progressing by "an almost continual series of small backward steps on the part of the North American... and an equal closing of the gap by the Latin American."

The problem is that, relatively speaking, Americans live in a noncontact culture. Partly, this is a product of our puritan heritage. Dr. Hall points out that we spend years teaching our children not to crowd in and lean on us. We equate physical closeness with sex so that when we see two people standing close together, we assume that they must be either courting or conspiring. And in situations where we ourselves are forced to stand very close to another person—on a crowded subway, for example, we're careful to compensate. We avert our eyes, turn away, and if actual body contact is involved, tense the muscles on the contact side. Most of us feel very strongly that this is the only proper way to behave.

Hall has suggested that the degree of closeness neatly expresses the nature of any encounter. In fact, he has hypothesized a whole scale of distances, each felt to be appropriate in the United States for a particular kind of relationship. Contact to eighteen inches apart is the distance for wrestling or lovemaking or for intimate talk—here, even a discussion of the weather becomes highly charged. At this range, people communicate not only by words but by touch, smell, body heat; each is aware of how fast the other is breathing, of changes in pallor or texture of the skin. One and a half to two and a half feet is the close phase of what Hall calls personal distance. It approximates the size of the personal-space bubble in a noncontact culture. Four to seven feet is close social distance. In an office, people who work together normally stand this far apart to talk. However, when a man stands four to seven feet from where his secretary is sitting and looks down at her, it has a domineering effect. Far-phase social distance, seven to twelve feet, goes with formal conversation, and desks of important people are usually big enough to hold visitors to this distance. Above twelve feet, one gets into public distance, appropriate for speechmaking and for very formal, stiff styles of speaking.

Other psychologists have been designing experiments based on Hall's observation of American proxemic behavior,④ and their evidence suggests that the way human beings space themselves may be determined not only by their culture and the particular relationships involved, but by other factors as well. At a crowded cocktail party, people necessarily stand closer together to talk, and experiments indicate that they also stand closer in a public place, such as a park or on the street. Adam Kendo suggests that in public people need to emphasize more strongly the fact that they're together—and so can lay claim to a certain small bubble of privacy. When two individuals stand closer together than their situation and the setting seem to warrant, it may be simply because they like each other. Psychological studies have shown that people choose to stand closer to someone they like than to someone they don't; that friends stand closer than acquaintances do, and acquaintances closer together than strangers. The evidence also indicates that, in intimate situations, introverts maintain slightly greater distances than extroverts, and that pairs of women stand closer to talk than do pairs of men.

The relative position an individual chooses can be a status signal. A group leader, for example, automatically gravitates to an end chair at a rectangular table. And it seems that the average jury, meeting to pick a foreman and seated around a rectangular table, is most apt to elect one of the two individuals who occupy end chairs; furthermore, the individuals who choose to sit in those chairs in the first place are generally people with a lot of social status, who proceed to take leading roles in the discussion.

Adam Kendon points out that any group of people, when standing and talking, assumes what he calls a configuration. If the shape is circular, it's a safe bet that everyone in the group is on a more or less equal footing. Noncircles tend to have a "head" position and the person in it is usually, formally or informally, the leader. Seating arrangements are almost always physically imposed in a classroom, and they can affect behavior. In a seminar, if students sit in a horseshoe shape, those at the sides participate less than those at the end, who can more easily make eye contact with the instructor. When the students sit in rows, those in the centre have more to say than do those at the side and, again easy eye contact seems to be the explanation.

Other studies have shown that when two people expect to compete, they will usually sit opposite one another; expecting to cooperate, they sit side by side; while for ordinary conversation, they sit at right angles. When negotiators from two corporations hold a meeting, the teams may automatically line up facing one another across the conference table. However, if the meeting is adjourned for lunch, the men are likely to sit in alternating chairs at the restaurant tables, each negotiator sandwiched between two men from the other corporation. Once the occasion is defined as a social one, individuals are as careful to mix as they were earlier not to mix.

Space communicates. When a number of people cluster together in a conversational knot—at a party, for example, or outdoors on a college campus—each individual expresses his position in the group by where he stands. By choosing a distance, he signals how intimate he wants to be; by choosing a location, such as the head spot, he can signal what kind of role he hopes to play. When the group settles into a particular configuration, when all the shifting around stops, it's a sign that nonverbal negotiations are over. All concerned have arrived at a general, if temporary, agreement on the pecking order and the level of intimacy that's to be maintained, and perhaps on other relationships as well.

Discussion

1. In groups discuss: Which of the following experimental results are true to Chinese proxemic behavior and which are not?

— Friends stand closer together than acquaintances.

— Acquaintances stand closer together than strangers.

— Introverts maintain slightly greater distances than extroverts.

— Pairs of women stand closer to talk than do pairs of men.

— People with a lot of social status generally sit in an end chair at a rectangular table.

— When students sit in rows, those in the center have more to say than those at the side.

— When two people expect to compete, they will sit opposite one another.

— When two people expect to cooperate, they sit side by side.

2. In groups, using examples, comment on the opinions in the last paragraph of Passage 2.

3. Where do you usually choose to sit in a classroom? Why? If a person decided to change where he or she normally sits, do you think the person's behavior would change?

Passage 3

Time

The varying attitudes toward time and its utilization held by the various cultures in the world means that serious misunderstandings may arise in intercultural communication unless those individuals involved are aware of, and sensitive to, a number of basic considerations.

Americans and others in the Western world are said to live in the present and the near future and hence plan carefully. Other cultures, such as in the Middle East or Asia, live in their ancient pasts or in the far distant future and hence do not plan so assiduously. To the Hindu and Buddhist this life is only one among countless lives yet to come, merely one dot in an endless serious of dots, so why plan?

Americans look upon time as a present, tangible commodity, something to be used, something to be held accountable for. They spend it, waste it, save it, divide it, and are stewards of it, just as if they were handling some tangible object. In order to use time well, they schedule the day and week and month carefully, set up timetables, and establish precise priorities. They prepare carefully for business conferences, for personal interviews, for group meetings of all types. This they assume to be an elementary aspect of efficiency. But some Arabs, Asian and others look on this as obsessiveness, and aggressiveness. Their lack of planning communicates to Westerners laziness, inefficiency, and untrustworthiness.

Americans expect an invitation to a dinner or a request for a date or for any other social event to be proffered reasonably far in advance. This shows evidence that the inviter really wanted to have the guests, and that it was not some last minute decision on his part dictated by factors other than his honest desire. To do otherwise would be considered an insult. In fact, often such last minute invitations, no matter how enticing, will be turned down basically because the recipient refuses to permit himself to be "secured" at the last minute. But in the Arab and Asian world, many simply forget appointments and arrangements if they are planned too far in advance, and their last minute invitations are sincere, and certainly not to be interpreted as insults.

The American divides up the day very precisely and communicates only during certain hours. He withholds communication during other hours, such as late at night or early in the morning, at which times only some emergency would initiate a telephone call, or a visit, to someone. But people of some other cultures do not divide the day so rigidly and are more liable to call at any time without being prompted by an emergency.

Americans place great stress on punctuality. Any consistently tardy person is taken to be undependable, untrustworthy, and disrespectful vis-à-vis the audience, message, or occasion.

For many situations Americans would consider tardiness of five minutes to be relatively serious and improper, but other cultures would consider such an attitude to be a rather neurotic slavery to time. Many Americans abroad could avoid much frustration if they realized that someone in another culture would have to be fifteen or even as much as forty-five minutes tardy if he were to be considered as late in his time framework as five minutes is in America's. In some cultures it is assumed that a busy, important person should come late. Hence, coming on time would only lower his prestige. Americans serving abroad have to clarify whether the beginning time of a scheduled meeting is to be "American" or "local" time.

Discussion

1. The verbal phrases of "time" in Passage 3 reveal that time seems to be handled as a tangible object (e. g. one can "gain time," "lose time," or even "kill time"). "Time" is sometimes treated as though it were a possession (e. g. "Do you have any time?" "Can you get some time for this?") Individually, list more expressions of time that reveal this idea and then compare your list with that of your partner's.

2. Discuss the following questions in groups:

— What do you think of careful planning for business conferences, personal interviews, and group meetings? Do you think of it as "obssessiveness" and "aggressiveness"?

— What's your opinion of some cultures' seeming lack of planning? Do you think it communicates laziness, inefficiency, and untrustworthiness? Why/Why not?

— What do you usually plan carefully in advance?

3. What are the usual Chinese customs with regard to the following?

— The most suitable time of day for visiting friends

— The most suitable time of day for making telephone calls to friends

— The amount of time that normally passes between a giving dinner party invitation and the dinner party

— An attitude toward tardiness: How late may a person be for an appointment without making an excuse or an explanation? (for a class, work, a meeting, a job interview, a dinner party, a date with a friend)

— An attitude toward visitors without prior notice

4. Summarize the different concept of time between Chinese and Western cultures by comparing your discussion and the information provided in Passage 3.

Kinesics[5]

Gestures, body movements, facial expressions, and eye contact are behaviors termed kinesics. In his landmark book Gestures, Desmond Morris (1979) wrote that communication depends heavily on the actions, postures, movements, and expressions of our bodies.

Morris and his colleagues studied the use of 20 of the most familiar European gestures to map their use across national boundaries. For example, they found the thumbs-up gesture commonly used in the United States by hitchhikers to be more widely understood to mean "okay."

Morris and his colleagues found wide variations even with such universal rituals as nodding agreement and greeting friends. Although most cultures do indicate "yes" by a nod of the head and "no" by shaking it, there are variations: In Ceylon, for example, a yes answer to a specific question is indicated by a nod of the head, whereas general agreement is indicated by a slow sideways swaying of the head.

For greetings, in the United States a handshake is appropriate. In France, where the traditional U. S. handshake is considered too rough and rude, a quick handshake with only slight pressure is preferred. In Latin America, a hearty embrace is common among men and women alike, and men may follow it with a friendly slap on the back. In Ecuador, to greet a person without a handshake is a sign of special respect. In India, the handshake may be used by Westernized citizens, but the preferred greeting is the namaste⑥—placing the palms together and nodding one's head. In Japan, the traditional form of greeting is a bow or several bows.

Likewise, waving good-bye varies among cultures. In Italy, Colombia, and China, people may wave good-bye by moving the palm and fingers back and forth, a gesture that more likely means "come here" in the United States. But in Malaysia, beckoning someone by moving the forefingers back and forth would be taken as an insult.

Even seemingly obvious gestures can be misunderstood. Using fingers to indicate numbers can vary. In the United States, most people would indicate "1" by holding up the forefinger. In parts of Europe, "1" is indicated by using the thumb, "2" by the thumb and forefinger.

The Japanese point their forefingers to their faces to indicate they are referring to themselves, whereas in the United States, citizens are more likely to point to their chests. And it is said that at least some Japanese women stick out their tongues to indicate embarrassment.

Patterns of eye contact learned in childhood seem to be relatively unaffected by later experiences. One study showed that Arabs, Latin Americans, and Southern Europeans focused their gaze on the eyes or face of their conversational partner, whereas Asians, Indians and Pakistanis, and Northern Europeans tend to show peripheral gaze or no gaze at all (Harper, Wiens, & Matatazzo, 1978). Duration of eye contact varies in diverse cultures (Shuter, 1979). In the United States, the average length of eye contact is 2.95 seconds, and the average length of time two people gaze at each other is 1.18 seconds (Argyle, 1998; Argyle & Ingham, 1972). Any less than that and we may think the person is shy, uninterested, or preoccupied. Any more than that and we may think the person is communicating unusually high interest.

Discussion

1. In small groups, give the interpretation of the following gestures discussed in Passage 4 in Chinese, American or British cultures.
— The thumb-up
— A handshake
— An embrace
— A friendly slap on the back
— A bow
— A gesture moving the palm and fingers back and forth
— Fingers used to indicate numbers
— A gesture pointing to oneself

2. English has common accompanying gestures that indicate meaning; for example, cross one's fingers for "Good luck," "Shh" with forefinger in front of the mouth is "to ask someone to be quiet." Demonstrate in class other common gestures you know about in English and give your interpretation.

3. In class, produce an inventory of common Chinese gestures.

Classroom Tasks

Task 1

Smiles display emotions and the whole world smiles, but the when and why of smiling differs from culture to culture. Read the following situation and discuss the questions.

A Chinese man, Mr. Wang had just started working in a new company in Australia. It was morning teatime and he was sitting in the tearoom smoking a cigarette. Suddenly one of his workmates came in and angrily pointed to a "No Smoking" sign. Mr. Wang was very embarrassed. He laughed and put his cigarette out. However, this did not seem to satisfy the man, who started to talk rapidly and angrily. Hoping to calm him down, Mr. Wang smiled and apologized, trying to explain that he had not noticed the sign.

Questions:

1. Do you think that Mr. Wang's apology is acceptable?

2. In your opinion, why was the Australian workmate so angry with Mr. Wang even after he put out his cigarette?

3. What would you advise the two participants to do in future to avoid the conflict?

4. Besides conveying emotions of happiness, does the smile display any other expressions in Chinese culture (Try to think when you usually smile)? Could the meanings attached to them cause any misunderstandings to Westerners?

Task 2

In small groups, discuss the cultural conflicts in the following cases and explain what has gone wrong.

Case 1: *Some Western speakers think that Chinese students don't pay much attention to their talks, because they tend to avoid direct eye contact to the speaker and don't like to raise questions at the end of the talk.*

Case 2: *Some Westerners think that Chinese people are cold because parents don't usually kiss their children, nor are husbands and wives seen to kiss each other when they meet after a long separation.*

Case 3: *Some Western researchers think that the silence of Easterners in communication shows a lack of confidence or communicatively apprehensive* (交际恐惧症), *especially when speakers don't answer questions, and listeners don't ask questions or don't respond.*

Task 3

Carry out a study on either of the following topics and give a presentation to the class.

— What is the prevalent attitude towards time in Chinese culture? How does it influence the pace of their life?

— Are there any perceptions about the use of time or space in Chinese culture that differ greatly from Western cultures?

Task 4

In small groups, discuss the following opinions.

Some researchers on time claimed:

— People living in a developed society have less free time than people living in a developing society.

— The pace of life in bigger cities is faster than that in smaller cities.

— The pace of life in a society that values individualism is faster than one that emphasizes collectivism.

Notes

① Passages 1 and 4 are extracted from Jandt, F. E., 1995, *Intercultural Communication: An Introduction*, California: Sage Publications Ltd, p. 87, pp. 77—79.

Passage 2 is extracted from Markstein, L. & L. Hirasawa, 1977, *Expanding Reading Skills*, Rowley: Newbury House Publishers, Inc, pp. 83—89.

Passage 3 is extracted from Jensen, J. V., "Perspective on Nonverbal Intercultural Communication," in 胡文仲 ed, 1990, *Selected Readings in Intercultural Communication*, 湖南教育出版社, pp. 132—136.

The passage in Task 1 is adapted from Brick, J., 1991, *China: A Handbook in Intercultural Communication*, Sydney: Macquarie University, p. 114.

② Samovar, L. A., R. E. Porter & L. A. Stefani, 2000, *Communication between Cultures*, Beijing: Foreign Language Teaching and Research Press, p. 149.

③ Edward T. Hall：美国人类学家。

④ proxemic behavior：体距行为。

⑤ kinesics：身势学。

⑥ namaste：(印度教)合十礼。

家 庭 观

　　家庭是社会的组成部分。一个家庭的组合形式、信仰、家规、习惯以及其成员的所思所想、所作所为无不受到传统、价值观等大的社会文化背景的影响。以农耕自然经济为基础的封建社会统治了中国几千年,封建宗法制度长期以来深深地影响着中华民族的生活,由此形成了民族心理的两大特点:重视血缘关系,强调等级差异。而在我们的日常生活和工作中强调孝敬长辈,尊重领导,在语言称谓使用中长幼有序,尊卑有别,则无不折射出民族文化心理。这与西方人崇尚个体主义,强调个人独立的价值取向有很大不同。这也就是我们中国人很难理解西方的年轻人18岁以后大多要在经济和情感上独立于父母,而老年人则倾向独自生活的原因所在。本单元提供了一些英美国家家庭的基本情况和课堂讨论,以启发学习者从民族心理的深层结构来对比和探讨中西方文化在家庭观念方面的差异及其根源。

Unit 4 [1]

Family Values

Families do not develop their rules, beliefs, and rituals in a vacuum. What you think, how you act, even your language, are all transmitted through the family from the wider cultural context. This context includes the culture in which you live, and those from which your ancestors have come.

——M. McGoldrick[2]

Reading and Discussion

The American Family

In the United States the nuclear family, which consists of the father, the mother, and the children, is considered "the family." The extended family, common in other cultures, includes grandparent, aunts, uncles, cousins, nephews, nieces, and in-laws. The distinction between the nuclear and extended family is important because it suggests the extent of family ties and obligations. In extended families the children and parents have strong ties and obligations to relatives. It is common in these families to support older family members, to have intensive contact with relatives, and to establish communal housing.

The American nuclear family usually has its own separate residence and is economically independent of other family members. Relatives are still considered "family" but are often outside the basic obligations that people have to their immediate families. When couples marry, they are expected to live independently of their parents and become "heads of households" when they have children. It is not unusual in times of financial need for nuclear family members to borrow money from a bank rather than from relatives. Grandparents, aunts, uncles, and cousins, then, are not directly involved in the same way as they would be in an extended family structure.

In both nuclear and extended families, the culture imposes set roles upon parents. Traditionally the male has been responsible for financial support of the home and family members. The female has often been responsible for emotional support, child raising, and housekeeping. However, among people in some parts of the United States these parental functions are no longer fixed. The prescribed role of the man as "breadwinner" and the woman as housewife is changing. These changes include working mothers, "househusbands," and an increasing number of daycare centers for children. Yet, traditional roles may be preserved even in households where the wife is working.

Now economic conditions, social attitudes, and job mobility in the United States compete with traditional influences. Changes in the American family structure are evidenced by increased rates of separation and divorce. In certain areas of the country these trends have resulted in a growing number of "single-parent" families, remarried parents, and communal lifestyles. This does not indicate, however, that the institution of marriage is crumbling. It is estimated that four out of five divorced couples eventually remarry other people. These shifts in family relationships may be interpreted as a breakdown or, alternatively, as an adaptation of the American family to changing roles, attitudes, and values. The changes, according to the more traditional viewpoint, represent a breakdown in the family structure, a disintegration of values, and a decline of morality. Others, who believe it is necessary to adapt to a rapidly changing society, believe these shifts in family structure are inevitable and positive.

Passage 2

Family Structure in Britain

The British live longer, marry later, have fewer children and are more likely to get divorced than ever before. Young people leave home earlier, though not necessarily to get married. More women now go out to work and more people, especially the old, live alone. The nuclear family (parents and perhaps two children) has largely replaced the extended family where several generations lived together.

Although patterns are changing, most people in Britain still get married and have children and stay together until the end of their lives. People are marrying later: the average woman gets married at twenty-four to a man who is just over two years older (although it is estimated that 40 per cent of couples live together before getting married). Mrs. Average now has her first child at the age of twenty-seven, but she will have only one or two children: only one mother in four has more. Nine out of ten married women will have children at some point in their lives. And despite the changes in working habits it is usually the woman who has overall responsibility for domestic life; the traditional division of family responsibilities still persists.

Britain has one of the highest divorce rates in Western Europe: approximately one in three marriages ends in divorce, half of them in the first ten years of marriage. As a result more people are getting remarried and there are now over a million single parents looking after 1.6 million children.

Discussion

1. Work in groups.

— Define the two basic types of families, the nuclear family and the extended family, and discuss advantages of each type.

— Why do you think American nuclear family members do not prefer to borrow money from their relatives when they are in need of money?

2. Discuss in groups: Which viewpoint do you agree with? Why?

— The changes represent a breakdown in the family structure, a disintegration of values, and a decline of morality.

— These shifts in family structure are inevitable and positive.

3. Describe the types of Chinese families found in either urban areas or the countryside to your class.

4. Discuss in class.

— What do you think are the distinct differences between Western and Chinese families?

— What are the factors that affect family values both in the West and in China?

Passage 3

The Elderly in America

The financial support of the elderly is often provided by social security or welfare systems which decrease dependence on their family. Additionally, older people may seek their own friends rather than become too emotionally dependent on their children. Senior citizens' centers provide a means for peer-group association within one's own age group. There are problems, however, with growing old in the United States. Glorification of youth and indifference to the aged have left many older people alienated and alone.

Some families send their old relatives to nursing homes rather than integrate them into the homes of the children or grandchildren. This separation of the elderly from the young has contributed to the isolation of an increasingly large segment of society. On the other hand, there are many old people who choose to live in retirement communities where they have the companionship of other older people and the convenience of many recreational and social activities close to home.

Discussion

1. Describe the life of the elderly in general in China to your class.

2. Discuss in groups: What family values are reflected in the treatment of the elderly both in Chinese and American cultures?

Passage 4

Youngsters in America

Acculturation, which begins at birth, is the process of teaching new generations of children the customs and values of the parents' culture. How people treat newborns, for example, can be indicative of cultural values. In the United States it is not uncommon for parents to put a newborn in a separate room that belongs only to the child. This helps to preserve parents' privacy and allows the child to get used to having his or her own room, which is seen as a first step toward personal independence. Americans traditionally have held independence and a closely-related value, individualism, in high esteem. Parents try to instill these prevailing values in their children. American English expresses these value preferences: children should cut the (umbilical) cord "and are encouraged not to be" tied to their mothers' apron strings. "In the process of their socialization children learn to" look out for number one and to "stand on their own two feet."

Many children are taught at a very early age to make decisions and be responsible for their actions. Often children work for money outside the home as a first step to establishing autonomy. Nine- or ten-year-old children may deliver newspapers in their neighborhoods and save or spend their earnings. Teenagers may babysit at neighbors' homes in order to earn a few dollars a week. Receiving a weekly allowance at an early age teaches children to budget their money, preparing them for future financial independence. Many parents believe that managing money helps children learn responsibility as well as appreciate the value of money.

Upon reaching an appropriate age (usually between 18 and 21 years), children are encouraged, but not forced, to "leave the nest" and begin an independent life. After children leave home they often find social relationships and financial support outside the family. Parents do not arrange marriages for their children, nor do children usually ask permission of their parents to get married. Romantic love is most often the basis for marriage in the United States; young adults meet their future spouses through other friends, at school, at jobs, and in organizations and religious institutions. Although children choose their own spouses, they still hope their parents will approve of their choices.

In many families, parents feel that children should make major life decisions by themselves. A parent may try to influence a child to follow a particular profession but the child is free to choose another career. Sometimes children do precisely the opposite of what their parents wish in order to assert their independence. A son may deliberately decide not to go into his father's business because of a fear that he will lose his autonomy in his father's workplace. This independence from parents is not an indication that parents and children do not love each other. Strong love between parents and children is universal and this is no exception in the American family. Coexisting with such love in the American family are cultural values of self-reliance and independence.

Discussion

1. In pairs work out the meaning of the following expressions:
    to cut the cord   to be tied to mother's apron strings
    to leave the nest   to stand on your own two feet

2. Work individually. At what age did (do, will) you start to do the following?

— live in your own room;

— earn your pocket money;

— make decisions by yourself, esp. major decisions in your life;

— leave home and live in your own place;

— receive a weekly (monthly) allowance and be able to budget the money.

Compare your answers with your partner's, explain your different answers to each other.

3. Work in groups. Suppose you have a child, when do you think it would be appropriate for him/her to do the things listed above?

4. Work in small groups. Do you agree with the following? Why/ Why not?

— Managing money helps children learn responsibility and appreciate the value of money.

— Children are encouraged to leave home between the ages of 18 and 21.

— Children do not need to ask permission of their parents to get married, but hope their parents will approve of their choices.

— Children should make major decisions by themselves.

— A son may not go into his father's business deliberately.

5. Describe the life of the young people in China to your group.

6. Cultures are classified, by some scholars, by the characteristics of individualism and collectivism. Generally speaking, Western cultures fall into the former, while Asian the latter.

Work in groups. Give examples of different behaviors, actions or ideas concerning family values between Westerners and Chinese that illustrate these two cultural patterns.

Classroom Tasks

Task 1

Individually, read the following letter written by an American student. Then work in pairs. Suppose one of you is the writer of the letter and the other is a Cultural Advisor. The letter writer poses the questions or problems first and then the Advisor gives advice. After the pair work, discuss the following questions in class:

— What problem is the writer of the letter experiencing?
— Why is the writer experiencing this problem?
— What differences in Chinese and Western values are shown concerning the situation in the letter?

Dear Cultural Advisor,

I have known M for the past year. He is a Chinese exchange student at our high school, and we have a lot of fun together. Now it's time for both of us go to college. I am going to study medicine, because I really want to be a doctor. My father was a little disappointed, because he always wanted me to be a lawyer. But both of my parents are happy for me since I have definite idea of what I want to do with my future.

I'm disappointed for M though. He really likes children and would love to be a teacher, but he will not study to become a teacher. Instead, he will study business and work in his family business in his country. That is what his family has always planned for him. I'm sorry that he is not able to do what he wants to do. I keep encouraging him to become a teacher, but he keeps telling me it's not that simple. We argue all the time over this issue. I just don't understand why he will not tell his family what he really wants to do. Can you please help me?

Task 2

This story tells of an incident in an American family in which a daughter goes against her parent's wishes. Wang Ying, a student from China, observes the situation. Read the story and then discuss the questions following the story.

Wang Ying: a Chinese student
Carol: Wang Ying's American friend
Dr. Turner: Carol's father
Mrs. Turner: Carol's mother

Wang Ying has been invited to the Turners' home for dinner. She is sitting at the table and is enjoying dinner and conversation with the family. During dinner the phone rings and Carol's younger brother answers it. The following conversation takes place:

Carol's Brother: Carol, it's Bill.

Mrs. Turner: (*surprisingly*) Bill? I thought you weren't seeing him any more, Carol.

Without replying, Carol leaves the room to answer the phone. When she returns, she silently continues her dinner.

Dr. Turner: Carol, was it Bill?

Carol: Yes.

Dr. Turner: Are you still seeing him even though we told you we didn't approve?

Carol: (*angrily*) Do I have to tell you everything? Listen, Dad, I know Bill doesn't have a college education but he is working for his brother in a construction company. He's trying to earn enough money to return to school. You always say that you respect hard-working people. Why shouldn't I see him any more?

Dr. Turner: (*softly but seriously*) I hope you're not serious about Bill, Carol. He promised to stay in college but he dropped out two times. Do you want to marry someone whose personality you'll have to change?

Mrs. Turner: Carol, Bill is different from us. We're only saying this because we love you. Bill just isn't your kind.

Carol: (*furious*) What do you mean, "my kind"? He's a human being! Just because he comes from a family that has less money than we do! What kind of democracy do you believe in? Everyone is supposed to be equal. He and his family are just as good as we are. (*By now, Carol is shouting loudly.*)

Wang Ying is feeling embarrassed and stares at her plate.

Carol's Brother: Come on, Mom and Dad. Bill is a nice guy.

Carol: Just because his parents are farmers who work with their hands and you are professors who work with your heads. What difference does that make?

Mrs. Turner: Carol, we're very disappointed in you. After all, we know what is best for you.

Suddenly Carol gets up, takes Wang Ying's arm, and pulls her to the door.

Carol: Come on, Wang Ying. Let's go to my room and study.

(*Carol and Wang Ying quickly walk out. Wang Ying tries to say to Carol's parents that she is sorry but Carol pulls Wang Ying away.*)

Discuss the following questions in groups.

— What were the problems between Carol and her parents?

— Who do you think was right?

— Would your family disagree in front of guests? Do you think any members of Carol's family were rude?

— How would your family deal with these types of problems if the problems exist?

2. Discuss the question in class: If your family deals with the problem differently, what do you think are the possible underlying reasons for the differences?

Task 3

1. Work in pairs. The following are some kinship terms in English. First give as many Chinese reference of the same terms as possible. For example, uncle: 伯伯, 叔叔, 舅舅, 姑父, 姨夫. Then discuss the difference in its classification between languages and cultures of the English-speaking countries and of China.

grandfather grandmother grandson granddaughter
aunt uncle nephew niece
cousin brother-in-law sister-in-law

2. Forms of address are different between English and Chinese. For example, in the West children occasionally call their parents, but especially their stepparents by their first names; college students call their teachers by their first names. In China, however, these are unacceptable.

In class discuss:

— differences in the forms of address between Chinese and English.

— Do you think there are any cultural reasons underlying these differences?

Task 4

In the conversation A and B are talking about relationships between children and parents. They seem not to be able to understand each other. Read the conversation and discuss the question in class.

A: I think it's terrible that in your country children leave their parents when they're so young. Sometimes what shocks me even more is that many parents want their children to leave home. I can't understand why children and parents don't like each other in your country.

B: In your country parents don't allow their children to become independent. Parents keep their children protected until the children get married. How are young people in your country supposed to learn about life that way?

What cultural values and beliefs are reflected in these two countries (e. g. what does each culture consider right and positive)?

Notes

① Passages 1, 3 and 4 are extracted from Levine, D. R. & M. B. Adelman, 1982, *Beyond Language: Intercultural Communication for English as a Second Language*, New Jersey: Prentice-Hall, Inc., Englewood Cliffs, pp. 91—92, p. 90, pp. 89—90.
Passage 2 is taken from Harvey, P. & R. Jones, 1992, *Britain Explored*, London: Longman, p. 88.
Task 1 is adapted from Matikainen, T. & C. B. Duffy, 2000, "Developing Cultural Understanding" in *Forum*, 38(3), p. 47.
Task 2 and Task 4 are adapted from Levine, D. R. & M. B. Adelman, 1982, *Beyond Language: Intercultural Communication for English as a Second Language*, New Jersey: Prentice-Hall, Inc., Englewood Cliffs, pp. 102—103, p. 180.
② McGoldrick, M., "Ethnicity and Cultural Diversity, and Normality," in F. Walalish, ed. 1973, *Normal Family Processes*, New York: Guilford Press, p. 331, cited from Samovar, L. A. et al, 2000, *Communication between Cultures*, Foreign Language Teaching and Research Press, p. 106.

教　育

"教育是整个社会大系统中的一个子系统。"一个国家的教育思想、学校建制、教学理念、学习风格、师生关系等无不受到其传统和文化的影响。譬如，在外籍教师的语言课堂上，这种现象尤为突出。外语课堂本身就是一个"跨文化实验室"。在走进这个实验室之前，无论是中国学生还是西方教师，对语言的本质、语言教与学的有效方法、教学大纲与教材的作用、教师与学生在课堂上各自所担负的角色和任务、师生关系等诸方面已有各自的一整套预设、想法和经历。中国学生从进入小学开始就受着一整套程式化课堂教学的熏陶。在学习过程中，学生对教材和教师的依赖性很强。而外籍教师普遍认同的教学方法为：课堂教学以学生为中心，学生应该积极参与课堂活动，亲身经历学习过程，通过不断尝试运用语言来学习语言。当中国学生进入外教的语言课堂，就会自觉不自觉地用自己所熟悉和习惯的教学模式来要求外籍教师，那么，误解和冲突将不可避免。本单元介绍了一些有关英美两国的教育制度、教学理念等方面的基本情况，编写了课堂活动，旨在引发学习者在这方面对中西文化进行对比、思考和讨论。

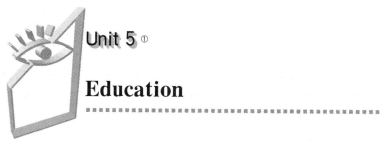

Unit 5 ①

Education

Very often certain values, attitudes, and behavioral patterns of the general culture are directly reflected in and reinforced by the educational setting. Cultural values, the role of the teacher, modes of learning, teacher-student interaction patterns, and norms of interaction must all be considered in cross-cultural analysis.

——*P. R. Furey*②

Reading and Discussion

The Education System in the UK

Education in the UK is compulsory for everyone between the ages of five and sixteen, and is provided by two kinds of schools: state-funded schools and independent (fee-charging) schools③. The UK has two distinct systems of courses and qualifications: one for England, Wales and Northern Ireland, and one for Scotland, each compatible with the other.

The structure of the education system in the UK has changed considerably over the recent years, reflecting successive governments' aims to improve quality, increase diversity and make institutions more accountable to students, parents, employers and taxpayers.

Pre-school education is available in both the independent and the state systems. Many children start their education at the age of three or four at a nursery school or in the nursery class at a primary school. The emphasis is on group work, creative activity and guided play. There is little or no teaching of special subjects or great emphasis on literacy and numeracy in early years.

Most UK children enter the state education system when they go to primary school at the age of five and generally move to secondary school at the age of eleven in England, Wales, and Northern Ireland and twelve in Scotland. In the independent system, preparatory (or primary) education is available for children aged five to thirteen. Many international students enter at the age of seven, often as boarders, and then transfer to a secondary school in the independent system when they are either eleven or thirteen.

All UK secondary schools, both state and independent, teach pupils at least until the age of sixteen and prepare them for GCSEs④ or equivalent qualifications. Compulsory education ends at age sixteen, though many pupils stay on beyond the minimum leaving age. About 90% of state secondary school pupils in England, Wales and Scotland go to district-based comprehensive schools, which provide a wide range of secondary education for most children of all abilities in the eleven to eighteen age range (twelve to eighteen in Scotland). In Northern Ireland and a few other areas of the UK, secondary education can be selected from grammar and secondary modern schools.

After completing compulsory education at the age of sixteen, students may legally leave school and start work. Most, however, study A-levels or equivalent qualifications as sixth-form students in a school, or attend a sixth-form college or college of further education. International students often enter the education system at this point, e.g. taking an A-level course in preparation for further or higher education in the UK.

Sixth-formers[5] usually finish their secondary education at the age of eighteen with A-levels or equivalent qualifications, then go on to study at either further or higher education level.

Further Education (FE) (including career based courses and some degree courses) is the term used to describe education and training that takes place after the school-leaving age of sixteen. Over six hundred FE colleges, both state-funded and independent, offer a very wide range of programmes, including English language courses, some GCSEs, A-levels and other equivalent, career based courses[6], access courses[7] and some degree courses.

Higher Education (HE) (including degree courses, postgraduate programmes and MBAs) is the term used to describe the education and training that takes place at universities, colleges and institutes offering studies at degree level and higher. The UK has over ninety universities and more than fifty HE colleges offering a wide range of courses, most of which lead to degrees or equivalent qualifications, postgraduate qualifications or MBAs.

Discussion

1. The system is decided by each local education authority in the UK, so it can vary. Passage 1 shows the usual system. Read the passage again and illustrate the organization of the education system in the UK with a chart. Compare your chart with your partner's and make some changes if necessary.

2. Work in pairs. Suppose your partner is a teacher from the

跨文化交际教程

UK. Describe the education system in China to your partner and together find out: In what ways does the Chinese state education system differ from that in the UK?

Coming of Age in the United States

In contrast to many of the world's societies, culture in the United States does not include a formal initiation through which young people pass from childhood to adulthood. Nevertheless, there are some cultural practices that signify maturity and some cultural contexts that have particular significance for the transition from youth to adulthood.

Among the middle class in the United States, an important part of coming of age for many people takes place in college. Anthropologist Michael Moffatt explored this process through a study of students at a major northeastern public university. These American students experienced the maturing process that takes place in college as a set of stages, corresponding with the freshman, sophomore, junior, and senior years. College freshmen were seen as foolish and inexperienced; sophomores were "wild men and women;" juniors saw themselves as suddenly having outgrown the juvenile behavior of the college dorm; and seniors were "burnt out," tired of college, and somewhat anxious about what would happen next.

Students attributed their growing maturity in college to both the formal and informal learning experiences of undergraduate life, but gave most importance to interaction with other students. They recognized that the academic aspect of college awarded the credentials needed to progress through a good career and contributed to broad general knowledge, but most students felt that it was extracurricular activity that most influenced their personal development. Some of this extracurricular activity was intellectual "fun": long discussions with their peers about political, philosophical, and ethical issues. But what students found most important in learning to be competent adults in the "real world" after graduation were the social skills they learned in informal interaction with their peers.

Foremost among these skills was the ability to take responsibility for oneself. College is a place where teachers and guidance councilors no longer monitor behavior, as in high school. Living away from home also means that parents do not know what the students are doing on a daily basis. With much more free time, a more flexible schedule, and many more distractions and activities available, students had to make their own decision about how to spend their time between work and play.

Discussion

1. Discuss in groups: Do you feel the same way as American students that in college
  — extracurricular activity influenced your personal development most?
  — social skills learned in informal interaction with peers were the most important?
  — foremost was the ability to take responsibility for oneself?
  — you had to make your own decision about how to spend your time?

2. What are your feelings or experiences in college life?

3. What is your expectation of your four-year college

experience in general (e. g. formal learning, academic success, personal development)?

4. Are there any differences between Chinese and American students in attitudes to learning and college experience? If there are, what values are shown in the differences?

Classroom Expectations

Participation in the American classroom is not only accepted but also expected of the student in many courses. Some professors base part of the final grade on the student's oral participation. Although there are formal lectures during which the student has a passive role (i. e., listening and taking notes), many courses are organized around classroom discussions, student questions, and informal lectures. In graduate seminars the professor has a "managerial" role and the students make presentations and lead discussions. The students do the actual teaching in these seminars.

Each teacher has his or her own style of teaching, and some teachers may use the "I speak, you listen" type lecture to give information to students. However, many teachers call on the student to participate in class, even in lecture classes.

Discussion is a cornerstone of the U. S educational system. It is a two-way activity; both the instructor and student must interact. Students need to generate ideas, offer examples, apply concepts, and ask questions. In a good discussion, the students and instructor have to maintain open minds. The U. S. education system strives to develop critical thinkers. You do not have to agree with every statement the professor makes and all comments by a professor are open to discussion. Respect plays an essential role in the system; student and teacher can respectfully disagree.

Such disagreement might seem risky and perhaps it is, but a free exchange of ideas is at the heart of American higher education. Professors can give you basic information from many different perspectives and then you must take that information and develop your own perspective.

Professors may also ask you to take more active roles in class. For example, dividing the class into smaller groups to carry out assignments is a popular method of instruction. American-trained teachers use small groups to help create a responsible, constructive, and helpful class environment so students will feel free to exchange ideas. Specifically, teachers might ask students to use the small group structure to:

- solve a problem;
- carry out class work in cooperation with others (students will often then have to present a group report to the whole class);
- "role play," which means to put oneself into another role such as mother, professor, or administrator and then act out a situation from that new perspective.

Usually, however, honest but non-hostile communication within the group can get the group working productively.

Role-playing is a learning technique most American students are very familiar with, as it is widely used at all levels of class instruction. Role-playing helps people learn to see a problem or situation from another's point-of-view.

In addition to class discussions and small group work, students will most likely be called on to give short speeches, prepare more formal presentations (often using visual aids), and take part in panel discussions in front of the class.

When students remain quiet in class they make it hard for the instructor to get to know them and their needs. Also, students become interested in each other as they listen to one another speak out in class. Quiet people can very easily be overlooked.

Many teachers believe that the responsibility for learning lies with the student. If a long reading assignment is given, instructors expect students to be familiar with the information in the reading even if they do not discuss it in class or give an examination. (Courses are not designed merely for students to pass exams.) The ideal student is considered to be one who is motivated to learn for the sake of learning, not the one interested only in getting high grades. Grade-conscious students may be frustrated with teachers who do not believe it is necessary to grade every assignment. Sometimes homework is returned with brief written comments but without a grade. Even if a grade is not given, the student is responsible for learning the material assigned.

When research is assigned, the professor expects the student to take the initiative and to complete the assignment with minimal guidance. It is the student's responsibility to find books, periodicals, and articles in the library or on-line. They expect students, particularly graduate students, to be able to exhaust the reference sources.

Professors will help students who need it, but prefer that their students not be overly dependent on them. (This differs from teacher-student relationships in other countries.) If a student has problems with classroom work, the student should either approach a professor during office hours or make an appointment.

Discussion

1. Passage 3 describes classroom participation at American universities. In groups comment on the teaching methods listed in

the passage (e. g. Do you think that they are helpful to students' learning?):

— Students make presentations;
— Students do the actual teaching;
— Students and the instructor have to maintain open minds;
— Students and the teacher can respectfully disagree;
— Homework is returned with comments, not a grade;
— In research students are expected to take the initiative and to exhaust the reference sources;
— Students should approach a professor during office hours or make an appointment with classroom problems.

2. In the same group, compare and discuss the attitudes to teaching and learning listed above and the attitudes and practice of Chinese teachers and students. Your discussion can be guided by the following questions:

— What classroom activities do you participate in?
— What value would you place on a seminar given by a classmate?
— What is the significance of classroom participation in your courses (e. g. Does it count in your final grade)?

3. "Group work" and "role play" are classroom techniques commonly used in Western countries. They are also frequently used in this course. In groups describe the characteristics of them and state the reasons why teachers in Western countries use them more than Chinese teachers.

4. Make a 2-minute presentation on the following topic: "The Responsibility for Learning Lies with the Students" (State whether or not you agree with the opinion and give your reasons).

Classroom Tasks

Task 1

The following situations are taken from a study of cross-cultural comparison. Read the situations and think over the questions individually by looking back on the time when you were at preschool. In groups, discuss the following questions. Then discuss Question 3 in class.

1. What do you think the Chinese teacher would do in Situations 1 & 2 in the context of a preschool in China?

2. What are the similarities and differences in preschool philosophies and practices regarding discipline, reward/punishment found in both the Western and Chinese preschools?

3. What values are emphasized in both the Western and the Chinese preschools?

Situation 1: *In an American preschool, when two boys, Mike and Stu, were fighting over blocks, the teacher separated both boys with her arms. After getting each boy to tell his side of the argument, the teacher said, "Let's not have any fighting; Mike, can you tell Stu what you want with words instead of grabbing?... Stu, when Mike took the block from you, how did you feel? Did you tell him that made you angry? Did you feel angry?"*

Situation 2: *In the American preschool, when a child, Kerry, would not put away the toys he played with after repeated exhortations, the teacher kneeled down, put her face directly in front of his, and repeated her command to clean up his blocks, reminding Kerry that each child is responsible for cleaning up the toys he or she uses. When Kerry still refused, the teacher made him sit on the "time-out" chair, to "think about it until you are ready to clean up."*

Situation 3: *In getting children ready for supper in the Chinese preschool, a teacher might say, "Now let's see. Who is sitting properly? How about Chen Ling—is he sitting properly? Who knows what is wrong with the way he is sitting? Should he be fiddling with his hands? Look at Lin Ping. Is she sitting nicely? See how straight her back is. See how she has her hands behind her back."*

Task 2

In groups read the following comments/situations and explain them by discussing:

— What assumptions do you think Australian and Chinese teachers/students bring to the class in the following situations?

— What are the Chinese and Western attitudes to learning and teaching?

— What is the role of the teacher and what is the role of the student in both the Chinese and the Western classrooms respectively?

The trouble with Chinese teachers is that they've never done any real teacher-training courses so they don't know how to teach. All they do is to follow the book. They never give us any opportunities to talk. How in the world do they expect us to learn?

Australian student in Shanghai 1988

Australian teachers are very friendly, but they often can't teach very well. I never know where they are going—there's no system and I just get lost. Also, they're often badly trained and don't really have a thorough grasp of their subject.

Chinese student in Sydney 1990

Task 3

The seating of students varies with the style of course, the number of students, and the instructor's teaching style in the Western classroom. Look at the differences between the seating arrangements in each of the following classroom, answer the questions individually, and then compare your answers with your partner's.

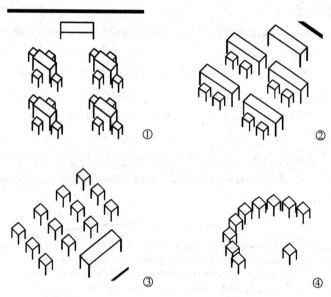

1. In your opinion, which classroom arrangement
   — is the most formal?
   — is the least formal?
   — encourages the most student participation?
   — enables students to have the most eye contact with the teacher?
   — is preferable for language learning?

2. Is there any difference in the classroom arrangement in your courses taught by Chinese teachers and foreign teachers?

3. Discuss the teaching principles that underlie the differences in teaching styles between Chinese and foreign teachers, such as classroom arrangement, the way of giving lectures, the method of organizing classroom activities, teacher/student relationship, student participation, etc.

Task 4

The theorists tell us that the characteristics of a good language learner are:

— confident in his/her ability to learn;
— self-reliant;
— motivated and enthusiastic;
— aware of why he/she wants to learn;
— unafraid of making mistakes, and unafraid of what he/she doesn't know;
— a good risk-taker;
— a good guesser;
— probably positive in his/her attitude to English language and culture;
— prepared to look for opportunities to come into contact with the language;
— willing to assume a certain responsibility for his/her own learning.

Make your own list of the characteristics a good language learner should have and compare yours with that of the theorists listed. In small groups explain your list to your group members and then each group should choose one student to make a speech on "A Good Language Learner" to the class.

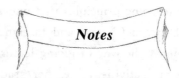

Notes

① Passage 1 is taken from http://www.britishcouncil.org/english.

Passage 2 is extracted from Nanda, S. and R. L. Warms, 1998, *Cultural Anthropology* 6th ed., Washington: Wadsworth Publishing Company, pp. 95—96.

Passage 3 is adapted from Levine, D. R. and M. B. Adelman, 1982, *Beyond Language—Intercultural Communication for English as a Second Language*, New Jersey: Prentice-Hall, Inc., pp. 111—113.

The material of three situations in Task 1 is taken from Nanda, S. and R. L. Warms, 1998, *Cultural Anthropology* 6th ed., Washington: Wadsworth Publishing Company, pp. 99—101.

Task 2 is adapted from J. Brick, 1991, *China: A Handbook in Intercultural Communication*, Sydney: Macquarie University, p. 153.

Task 3 is adapted from Levine, D. R. and M. B. Adelman, 1982, *Beyond Language—Intercultural Communication for English as a Second Language*, New Jersey: Prentice-Hall, Inc., pp. 169—170.

② Furey, P. R., "A Framework for Cross-Cultural Analysis of Teaching Methods," in *Teaching across Cultures in the University ESL Program*, edited by Patricia Byrd, Nat'l Assoc. for Foreign Students Affairs, 1986.

③ independent school：私立学校。

④ GCSE (General Certificate of Secondary Education)：普通教育证书,是英国完成中等教育的考试,也是参加大学入学考试的资格考试,分程度高的 A 级(A-level)和普通程度的 O 级(O-level)。

⑤ sixth-former：中学六年级学生。
⑥ career based course：职业培训课程。
⑦ access course：补习课程。

工 作 观

不同的文化推崇不同的工作理念。工作理念在工作的动力中占有重要的位置,同时在很大程度上影响着人们对工作所持有的价值观。深深植根于西方社会的工作理念受其历史、宗教、地理环境等因素的影响。人们相信只要努力工作,就会有所成就。物质上获得成功意味着得到上帝的宠爱,追求物质享受,拥有财富是上帝的旨意。由于持有这样的工作理念,人们对工作怀有很强的愿望和激情,常常通过工作中取得的成就来证明个人价值。本单元提供的阅读文章和课堂讨论,旨在引导学习者从中西方文化的深层角度,对在这两种文化背景下人们对工作的态度、员工与公司的关系、公司对员工的要求、员工变换工作的频率、管理层对变换工作的看法等方面的异同进行对比和分析。

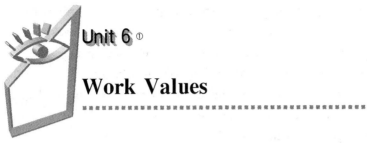

Unit 6 [1]

Work Values

The work ethic is a cultural norm that places a positive moral value on doing a good job and is based on a belief that work has intrinsic value for its own sake.

——Cherrington et al. [2]

Reading and Discussion

You Are What You Do

There is a popular saying, "You are what you eat," and although there may be some truth in that, in the United States a more appropriate saying is "You are what you do." In that country an individual is often judged by what he or she does for a living. And the more they do and the faster they do it, the better!

At social and professional gatherings it is not unusual for a guest to find him- or herself in the midst of many strangers, and people are expected to introduce themselves and to strike up conversations. The "How do you do?" is often followed by "What do you do?"

In the United States people try to prove their worth as human beings through their achievements. A person's job provides self-identification more than his or her family name or background. They encourage and stand in awe of the self-made person who has gone from rags to riches, the person who has "made it," not on the basis of family name but by his or her own efforts. In the United States there is a belief that people are rewarded for working, producing, and achieving. Many people believe that there is equality of opportunity that allows anyone to become successful. There are some people who do succeed in raising their economic and social levels. "Upward (occupational) mobility" or "climbing the ladder" are terms that refer to one's advancement in work. Many employees have a succession of jobs that constitute a career. Some businesses, organizations, government agencies, and firms provide employees with the opportunities to progress to higher positions. Promotions and increased responsibility generally bring higher salaries. Rewards for achievement in work are personal as well as financial. There is increased job satisfaction when employees have the opportunity to develop creative and intellectual skills. Gaining recognition from fellow workers, supervisors, and managers gives one a sense of importance and identity in society. These values help produce many workaholics—people who are addicted to their work—but this is not to say that Americans don't enjoy their leisure time. They do, but they usually keep leisure separate from work. Many of them like to both work hard and play hard.

Such an achievement-oriented society is bound to produce plenty of competition, because it is only by competing with others for the slice of the pie that people win success. The negative effects of a competitive society can be seen in their often strained interpersonal relations. These arise because in any competitive situation, someone has to lose. For every American who fits this mold, you can find one who doesn't. Not all Americans fit into the mainstream; some remain outside by choice and others because of circumstances beyond their control. For every person who does like to work, you can find one who doesn't. Each type contributes to the diversity of American culture.

In some nations it is considered disloyal to quit a job; deep reciprocal loyalties exist between employee and employer. Lifelong job security and family honor are frequently involved. This is not true in the United States. "Job-hopping" is part of the constant mobility. Americans consider it a "right" to be able to better themselves, to move upward, to jump from company to company if they can keep qualifying for most responsible (and therefore better) jobs.

The employer may be quite content too. Perhaps he has had the best of that man's thinking; a new person may bring in fresh ideas, improved skills, or new abilities. Then, too, a newcomer will probably start at a low salary for he will have no seniority. Hopping is so readily accepted, in fact, that a good man may bounce back and forth among two or three corporations, being welcomed back to his original company more than once through his career, each time at a different level.

Discussion

1. As a class, using examples, discuss the opinion, "You are what you do."

2. Work individually. Summarize the work attitudes and beliefs in the United States described in Passage 1. Then compile a list of them in the class. For example: If one works hard, he/she can become successful.

3. Passage 1 illustrates the American attitudes toward job mobility. In small groups discuss the Chinese attitudes toward job

mobility: e. g. what obligations do employers and employees have toward each other? How long do employees hope to stay in one job in general?

4. In groups discuss: What are the differences in work ethic, beliefs and attitudes toward work in China and the United States (considering the history, economy, society, values and social practice of the two nations)? Then each of you should give a short presentation on the topic to the class. (Do some research for your presentation.)

Passage 2

Employee Turnover[③]

Researchers wondered about the difference between employee turnover in cultures in the East and the West. They thought that the importance of the individual in Western culture might lead to a positive attitude concerning leaving employment. They were right. Overall, the researchers found that British employees have a much stronger positive attitude about quitting employment than do the Japanese. However, it was interesting to note that British employees were found to have a greater commitment to the organization where they worked than did the Japanese employee. They had a significantly greater acceptance of organizational goals and desire to maintain an employment relationship with their employer.

The researchers found that Japanese employees' feelings about others' opinions of their leaving a job were important in predicting employees' lack of turnover intentions. Japanese employees were less likely to consider leaving their present job if they thought that their family, colleagues, spouse or supervisor did not want them to, while the opinions of others appeared to make little impact on British employees' turnover intentions.

In the West individualism is paramount. Thus, in the West it does not matter what others think about one's decision to change jobs. Intentions to leave a job are mostly centered on what the employee thinks rather than what is expected or wanted by others. In Japan the converse was found to be true. Because cultures in the East are generally characterized by social interdependence what others think, need or want is important to the self-concept. Therefore, what others think plays largely in decisions such as leaving an organization to take a job elsewhere.

Employees who have a greater acceptance of organization goals and values and are willing to exert effort toward these goals have a greater desire to remain with the organization. This was true in both countries. However, this commitment was stronger among the British employees who tended to more strongly rate their identification with the places where they worked than did the Japanese worker.

While employers in the West may have the advantage of strongly committed employees, as long as the employee is with the organization, Japanese industry has the advantage of the "group think" aspects of their culture. Absenteeism and turnover are lower in Japan and the Japanese work longer hours than in the West. Since belonging to a company is important to the Japanese worker, Japanese industry has the advantage of a dedicated work force that is unlikely to leave, thus reducing training costs and improving quality through consistency.

跨文化交际教程

Work in groups.

— List differences in attitudes between British and Japanese cultures concerning leaving employment.

— List similarities in attitudes of Chinese and Japanese employees concerning leaving a job.

— Explain the following situations in employee turnover in values, beliefs and the work ethic of Britain and Japan.

• British employees have a stronger positive attitude about quitting employment.

• British employees have a greater commitment to the organization.

• The opinions of others make little impact on British employees' turnover intentions.

• Japanese employees think about others' opinions regarding leaving a job.

• Japanese work longer hours.

• In Japan employee turnover is lower.

The Future of Work

Futurist author Alvin Toffler approaches "The Future of Work" in terms of "great waves of change." The First Wave was the agricultural revolution that occurred over thousands of years, forming the basis for organized society. The Second Wave was the rise of industrialization within the last few hundred years creating the "smokestack" world in which we have grown up. The Third

Wave is a post-industrial trend led by high-technology, information-based services, and more flexible and responsive management practices that radically affects the foundations of an industrial society, and thus one's personal and social life is based upon these foundations. The Third Wave is just now emerging and will significantly change the world within the span of a few decades. As a result of this accelerating move into the Third Wave, Toffler foresees a radical reorganization of the economy and of employment trends.

As some traditional opportunities disappear, new ones will arise. There will be more emphasis upon working smarter instead of working harder. Where muscle-power was once the source of increased productivity, in the modern workplace mind-power will be the source. Widespread and instantaneous access to huge stores of information, the development of technology to manipulate this information, and the skills needed to master the technology and utilize the resulting output are all elements dependent upon efficient use of the mind. Third Wave industries will be knowledge-based ventures. In re-inventing the corporation, Naisbitt observes that in the new information society, the key resource has shifted [from capital] to information, knowledge, creativity. Naisbitt also sees a trend toward "self-management" among knowledge workers, eliminating the need for layers of administrative managers. He also makes the point that "self-management presumes independence, self-confidence, and competence, values which are increasingly important in the new worker."

Many more workers in the future will be "mind-workers." These workers will have specialized skills and knowledge. Toffler describes these workers as "more independent, more resourceful... better educated... used to change, ambiguity, flexible organization." He also sees the need for many workers with "people skills" to meet the need for training, retraining, employee relations, management, organizing, negotiating, and communicating.

Training and retraining will become much more important. Many workers who lose their jobs will never regain the positions they lost. They will be in the position of requiring significant retraining in order to qualify for other skilled employment. Many major corporations have recognized this trend, and have developed effective in-house retraining programs that allow displaced workers to move to different positions within the corporation. Even those workers who are not displaced will have to participate in ongoing training programs to maintain their skills in the fast-paced Third Wave industries. One study of this trend, "Schools of the Future," states that "in the future, worker's jobs will change dramatically every 5 to 10 years." This same study foresees a partnership between business and education, aimed at increasing the relevance and responsiveness of education to the ever-changing demands of the workplace. Training is even more important for those with marginal employability.

Discussion

1. Work in groups. On the basis of the economy and employment trends foreseen by Alvin Toffler, work out a list of qualities a future worker should have (e. g. learning to listen and speaking effectively; ability to work with people).

What qualities are already required for employees now?

2. In groups try to predict a possible partnership between education and the ever-changing demands of the workplace in the near future (in 20 years). Report your discussion to the class.

3. Do you think that Chinese values and Western values are

becoming more similar or increasingly different in the future of work? Why?

Classroom Tasks

Task 1

Mr. Jiang applied for a job as a computer programmer in a large Australian computing company. As he was very well qualified in computing and had extensive experience, he thought that he had a very good chance of getting the job. He was interviewed by three people who started out by asking him questions about his qualifications and experience. He answered confidently.

Suddenly, however, one of the interviewers asked him whether he could work in a team. Mr. Jiang was rather surprised at the question but said "Yes." He was then asked why he was interested in this particular job. He explained that the job was very suitable for him as he had done similar work before. He also explained that the salary was better than the salary he was currently receiving. Finally, he was asked if he himself had any questions. He did not.

Mr. Jiang left the interview feeling that he had done well. However, he did not get the job and later found out that the successful applicant had less experience than he had.

Read the situation individually and then discuss the questions in groups.

— Why do you think Mr. Jiang didn't get the job? What are the characteristics valued by Australian employers?

— If the company were a Chinese company, do you think it would have been possible for Mr. Jiang to get the job? What characteristics do Chinese managers and directors value in their subordinates?

— In what way do the two systems (Australian and Chinese) differ?

Task 2

The following are advertisements taken from the Employment Section of American (A—D) and Chinese (E—F) newspapers (The names of the companies are fictitious and some phone numbers and email addresses have been omitted, but the other information is taken from real ads.). After reading these ads, discuss the questions.

A. DOM needs Software Engineers and Programmer Analysts

DOM is the leader in computer systems for the publishing industry. The unstructured yet supportive environment offers personal and professional freedom. We are looking for independent, innovative people who will enjoy the excitement of a product-oriented environment and who want to be highly visible members of end-user software development teams. Bring your proven track record④ of project accomplishment and high productivity to us. DOM REWARDS RESULTS!!

B. Art Director

We need an aggressive, sales-oriented, creative graphic arts person with at least 3 years agency-type exp. Must be fully familiar with all aspects of commercial printing. Should want to take charge and manage a small staff with an eye on bottom-line performance. Salary up to $28,000 based on experience. Send resume: KOPCO Printing Inc. Box 25.

C. Copy Director for Ad Agency

We're looking for a dynamic and creative writer/leader to head up a staff of talented writers. You should be able to direct this pool of raw talent, teaching them how to think conceptually in all media—from Broadcast and Print to Direct Mail and promotional material. In addition to being an excellent "wordsmith" yourself with an enviable track record, you should be able to look at the big picture and plan your concepts to cross into other media. Marketing skills or a good business sense are essential, plus the ability to think on your feet at client meetings. Please send resume and salary history to this top-notch agency at Box 666.

D. Fast-Food Managers

We are expanding our operations, and in order to do this we must hire aggressive, hard-working individuals who are looking toward the future. Openings are now available. Call 555—6677.

E. Now Hiring Asia Sales Manager

A world market leader in the manufacturing of component parts of electrical appliances is looking for a Sales Manager for Asia. Applicants should be:

- Fluent in English and Mandarin
- Educated in engineering or related technical field
- 5+ years' technical sales experience
- Able to develop and implement a Sales and Marketing Plan
- Able to assist clients with technical aspects of production
- Willing to relocate to China and travel regularly in Asia
- Available to begin in March or April 2003

Submit a resume or request a complete job description before Feb 14 to:

phone: ...

fax: ...

email: ...

F. Job Vacancy—General Manager

In order to expand operating scale, to continuously develop towards globalization, NHL has established a Hydraulic Cylinder Precision Machinery Co., and now is openly recruiting a General Manager.

Basic requirement: Good moral quality, previous experience in the management and operation of a modern hydraulic components manufacturing facility.

Remuneration: Annual salary is 40,000 US dollars for a foreigner (after tax).

Application method: The candidate must provide his ideas and plans for company development, and attend a question & answer session for the bidding of the job (Company information can be obtained from the Internet, or call us so that we can mail you the requested information).

Once employed, the GM will be a legal representative of the fully invested subsidiary under NH, and be responsible for the operation & management approach, planning and development of the Hydraulic company.

Application: via Internet or telephone calls, with a copy of your resume.

Contact: ...
Tel: ...
Fax: ...
Website: ...
E-mail: ...

Discussion

1. Read the advertisements individually and put the relevant information in the ads into three lists: ①formal qualifications (degree, diploma, etc.); ②experience; ③personal characteristics.

2. Discuss the following questions in small groups, with the help of the information you got from Question 1 and then report your discussion to the class.

— Which is more important, experience or qualifications, for

American and Chinese employers respectively?

— Are there any general characteristics that all employers seem to be looking for?

— Are there any special characteristics listed above in American or Chinese advertisements?

— Do you find any evidence that illustrates "American work values" and "Chinese work values" in job ads? (You may like to include job advertisements from Chinese local newspapers.)

Task 3

The following "Work Values Inventory" describes a variety of satisfactions that people obtain from their jobs in Western societies. If an occupation does not match an employee's most important values (four or five) well, he/she will probably not be satisfied with it. Now read the inventory and list your own five most important values when you consider an occupation (You may include some values from the following). Present them to your group and discuss your work values.

— Help society: Do something to contribute to the betterment of the world I live in.

— Help others: Be involved in helping other people in a direct way, either individually or in small groups.

— Public contact: Have a lot of day-to-day contact with people.

— Work with others: Have a close working relationship with people as a result of my work activities.

— Competition: Engage in activities which pit my abilities against others where there are clear win-and-lose outcomes.

— Work under pressure: Work in situations where time pressure is prevalent and/or the quality of my work is judged critically by supervisors, customers or others.

— Power and authority: Control the work activities or

(partially) the destinies of other people.

— Work alone: Do projects by myself, without any significant amount of contact with others.

— Creativity: (general) Create new ideas, programs, organizational structures or anything else not following a format previously developed by others.

— Stability: Have a work routine and job duties that are largely predictable and not likely to change over a long period of time.

— Security: Be assured of keeping my job and a reasonable financial reward.

— Adventure: Have work duties which involve frequent risk-taking.

— Location: Find a place to live which is conducive to my life style and affords me the opportunity to do things I enjoy most.

— Profit-gain: Have a strong likelihood of accumulating a large amount of money or other material gain.

— Advancement: The opportunity to work hard and make rapid career advancement.

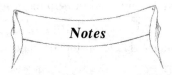

Notes

① Passage 1 is extracted from Irving, K. J., 1986, *Communicating in Context: Intercultural Communication Skills for ESL Students*, New Jersey: Prentice-Hall, pp. 116—117 and Lainer, A. R., 1981, *Living in the U. S. A.*, Chicago: Intercultural Press Inc., pp. 26—27.

Passage 2 is extracted from Hrzone, "Cultural Differences in Employee Turnover," http://www.hrzone.com.

Passage 3 is extracted from http://web.fccj.org. Task 1 is

adapted from Brick, J., 1991, *China: A Handbook in Intercultural Communication*, Sydney: Macquarie University, pp. 82—83.

Task 2 is adapted from Irving, K. J., 1986, *Communicating in Context: Intercultural Communication Skills for ESL Students*, New Jersey: Prentice-Hall, pp. 141—143.

The information of Task 3 is extracted from http://www.saf.ukplatt.edu.

② http://www.coe.uga.edu

③ employee turnover: 人事变动。

④ track record: 工作经历。

生　意　观

　　一个民族的历史、传统、价值取向对其生意观有着深远的影响。譬如：谈判的首要任务是签订合同，还是建立良好的关系，谈判中的措辞是直率还是委婉，说话风格是正式还是随意，生意态度是竞争还是双赢等；什么样的广告能耐人寻味，吸引顾客；怎样大小、颜色的产品包装能投顾客所好，适合销售；什么样的方式有利于产品促销等。经济全球化是一把双刃剑，巨大的潜在市场的另一方面是对你能否理解全新的文化环境的挑战。因此，最成功的跨国公司是那些其员工既懂得经济和国际竞争，又能够与别国合作者进行有效交流的公司。东西方文化差异较大，而这些差异在商务活动中显得尤为突出。本单元收入和编写了一些相关的文章和课堂讨论，以启迪学习者在这方面的思考和探讨。

Unit 7 ①

Business Attitudes

The most successful firms in the global arena will be companies whose employees not only understand world economics and global competitiveness but who also have the ability to communicate effectively with international counterparts. ②

Reading and Discussion

Other Cultures Are Not Like Yours

Today's world is drastically different from that of twenty, or even ten years ago. The influence of multinational corporations, the technological revolution, the "Information Superhighway," and the movement of the private and public sectors towards globalization, sets the scene.

New laws, agreements and regional partnerships—from NAFTA③ and GATT④ to the European Union and ASEAN⑤— have contributed to make this massive change not only possible but also achievable. This development demands a completely new approach to business or to any type of international relations. Globalization could be a two-edged sword. The opposite side of immense potential markets is the challenge of understanding or *misunderstanding an entirely new cultural milieu.*

   No matter who you are or where you live, no matter what nation or culture you come from, you will need to recognize one very important truth when you do business with colleagues in other countries. Other people—although they may dress like you, speak your language, or even work for the same company—are not "just like you." You'll do business with people that have very different histories, languages, and ways of doing business. They will have a different sense of time, and a different sense of humour. They will have different ways of negotiating, and different perceptions of when a deal has truly been made. They will also have different expectations of what it means to follow through on commitments and agreements.

   When you do business with companies in other countries, you are not just staying in a different hotel, eating a different meal, and meeting in different offices. You are entering someone else's world, and you need to understand the history of its people, the rules the culture runs by, and the way they view the business process. Every business traveler should know something about the country they are visiting—its history, its people, its heritage. It helps you make conversation, helps you learn more from the experience, and is a sign of respect for those you are meeting.

   Conducting international business in general and international marketing in particular demands sensitivity to cultural differences in behavior and expectation. Vast differences in cultural norms determine what is considered proper and tasteful advertising, what are appropriate colors for packaging, what are the most appealing sizes of units offered for sale, and what are the most effective means of promoting a product. Practices vary greatly. What is understood to be a token of regard in one country may be deemed a bribe in another.

Once you understand the basic facts about a culture, and something about its social rules, you are ready to do business. When does *yes* mean *yes*? When does *maybe* mean *no*? When should you raise the issue of payment? How are commitments followed through? — In order to get the best results, you need to know how business is done in your partner's culture. Social issues form the backbone of any culture. People in different countries conduct their lives in different ways: Which color flowers to bring? Which hand to shake? How to address your colleagues? Who speaks first? It is far better to know the rules than to risk offending anyone and losing a deal.

Discussion

1. In small groups interpret and discuss the following ideas.
— Globalization could be a two-edged sword.
— When you do business with companies in other countries (or do business via fax, telephone or internet while based in your own country) you are entering someone else's world.
— What is a token of regard in one country may be deemed a bribe in another.
— When does yes mean yes?
— When does maybe mean no?

2. Individually, list cultural differences (including those mentioned in Passage 1 and your own ideas) that may affect business success, e. g. the way of address, roles of politeness, respect, direct confrontation. Then, in small groups, compare your list with your group members' and give an explanation of your ideas which are different from others.

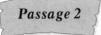

The Top Ten Ways Culture Affects Negotiating Style

Negotiation practices differ from culture to culture and as such culture can influence "negotiating style"—the way persons from different cultures conduct themselves in negotiating sessions.

The great diversity of the world's cultures makes it impossible for any negotiator, no matter how skilled and experienced, to understand fully all the cultures that he or she may encounter. How then should an executive prepare to cope with culture in making deals in Singapore this week and Seoul the next? One approach is to identify important areas where cultural differences may arise during the negotiation process. A knowledge of those factors may help a negotiator to understand a counterpart from another culture and to anticipate possible sources of friction and misunderstandings.

(1) Negotiating Goal: Contract or Relationship?

Different cultures may view the very purpose of a business negotiation differently. For many American executives, the goal of a negotiation, first and foremost, is to arrive at a signed contract between the parties. Americans consider a signed contract as a definitive set of rights and duties that strictly binds the two sides and determines their interaction thereafter.

Japanese, Chinese, and other cultural groups in Asia, it is said, often consider that the goal of a negotiation is not a signed contract, but the creation of a relationship between the two sides. Although the written contract describes the relationship, the essence of the deal is the relationship itself.

(2) Negotiating Attitude: Win/Lose or Win/Win?

Because of differences in culture or personality, or both, persons appear to approach deal making with one of two basic attitudes: that a negotiation is either a process in which both can gain (win/win) or a struggle in which, of necessity, one side wins and the other side loses (win/lose). Win/win negotiators see deal making as a collaborative and problem-solving process; win/lose negotiators see it as confrontational. In a reflection of this dichotomy, negotiation scholars have concluded that these approaches represented two basic paradigms of the negotiation process: ①distributive bargaining (i. e. win/lose) and ② integrative bargaining or problem-solving (i. e. win/win). In the former situation, the parties see their goals as incompatible, while in the latter they consider themselves to have compatible goals. The Chinese and Indians, in the survey, claimed that negotiation was for them win/win.

(3) Personal Style: Informal or Formal?

Personal style concerns the forms a negotiator uses to interact with counterparts at the table. Culture strongly influences the personal style of negotiators. It has been observed, for example, that Germans have a more formal style than Americans. A negotiator with a formal style insists on addressing counterparts by their titles, avoids personal anecdotes, and refrains from questions touching on the private or family life of members of the other negotiating team. An informal style negotiator tries to start the discussion on a first-name basis, quickly seeks to develop a personal, friendly relationship with the other team, and may take off his jacket and roll up his sleeves when deal making begins in earnest. Each culture has its own formalities, and they have special meaning within that culture. While nearly 83% of the Americans considered themselves to have an informal negotiating style, only

54% of the Chinese, 52% of the Spanish, and 58% of the Mexicans were similarly inclined.

(4) Communication: Direct or Indirect?

Methods of communication vary among cultures. Some groups place emphasis on direct and simple methods of communication; others rely heavily on indirect and complex methods. It has been observed, for example, that whereas Germans and Americans are direct, the French and the Japanese are indirect. Persons with an indirect style of communication often make assumptions about the level of knowledge possessed by their counterparts and to a significant extent communicate with oblique references, circumlocutions, vague allusions, figurative forms of speech, facial expressions, gestures and other kinds of body language. In a culture that values directness such as the American or the Israeli, one can expect to receive a clear and definite response to proposals and questions. In cultures that rely on indirect communication, such as the Japanese, reaction to proposals may be gained by interpreting seemingly indefinite comments, gestures, and other signs.

(5) Sensitivity to Time: High or Low?

Discussions of national negotiating styles invariably treat a particular culture's attitudes toward time. So it is said that Germans are always punctual, Latins are habitually late, Japanese negotiate slowly, and Americans are quick to make a deal.

(6) Emotionalism: High or Low?

Accounts of negotiating behavior in other cultures almost always point to a particular group's tendency or lack thereof to display emotions. According to the stereotype, Latin Americans show their emotions at the negotiating table, while Japanese and many other Asians hide their feelings. Obviously, individual personality plays a role here. There are passive Latins and hotheaded Japanese. Nonetheless, various cultures have different rules as to the appropriateness and form of displaying emotions, and these rules are brought to the negotiating table as well. The Latin Americans and the Spanish were the cultural groups that ranked themselves highest with respect to emotionalism in a clear statistically significant fashion. Among Europeans, the Germans and English ranked as least emotional, while among Asians the Japanese held that position, but to a lesser degree than the two European groups.

(7) Form of Agreement: General or Specific?

Cultural factors may also influence the form of the written agreement that parties try to make. Generally, Americans prefer very detailed contracts that attempt to anticipate all possible circumstances and eventualities, no matter how unlikely. Why? Because the "deal" is the contract itself, and one must refer to the contract to handle new situations that may arise in the future. Other cultures, such as the Chinese, prefer a contract in the form of general principles rather than detailed rules. Why? Because, it is claimed, the essence of the deal is the relationship between the parties. If unexpected circumstances arise, the parties should look to their relationship, not the details of the contract, to solve the problem.

(8) Building an Agreement: Bottom Up or Top Down?

Related to the form of the agreement is the question of whether negotiating a business deal is an inductive or a deductive process. Does it start from agreement on general principles and proceed to specific items, or does it begin with agreement on specifics, such as price, delivery date, and product quality, the sum total of which becomes the contract?

Different cultures tend to emphasize one approach over the other. Some observers believe that the French prefer to begin with agreement on general principles, while Americans tend to seek agreement first on specifics. For Americans, negotiating a deal is basically making a series of compromises and trade-offs on a long list of particulars. For the French, the essence is to agree on basic principles that will guide and indeed determine the negotiation process afterward. The agreed-upon general principles become the framework, the skeleton, upon which the contract is built.

(9) Team Organization: One Leader or Group Consensus?

In any international negotiation, it is important to know how the other side is organized and makes decisions. Culture is one important factor that affects the way groups are organized and the way organizations function. Some cultures emphasize the individual while others stress the group. These values may influence the organization of negotiating teams. One extreme is the negotiating team with a supreme leader who has complete authority to decide all matters. Many American teams tend to follow this approach, which has been labeled the "John Wayne⑥ style of negotiations." Despite the Japanese reputation for consensus arrangements, only 45% of the Japanese respondents claimed to prefer a negotiating team based on consensus. The Brazilians, Chinese, and Mexicans, to a far greater degree than any other groups, preferred one-person leadership, a reflection perhaps of the political traditions in those countries.

(10) Risk Taking: High or Low?

Research indicates that certain cultures are more risk averse than others. In deal making, the culture of the negotiators can affect the willingness of one side to take "risks" in a negotiation—to divulge information, try new approaches, or tolerate uncertainties in a proposed course of action. The Japanese are said to be highly risk averse in negotiations, and this tendency was affirmed by the survey. Americans, by comparison, considered themselves to be risk takers, but an even higher percentage of French, British, and Indians claimed to be risk takers.

This article reports and confirms what numerous other surveys have studied and observed: that culture can influence the way in which persons perceive and approach certain key elements in the negotiating process. A knowledge of these cultural differences may help negotiators to better understand and interpret their counterpart's negotiating behavior and to find ways to bridge gaps created by cultural differences.

Discussion

1. Summarize the negotiating style of Asian and the Western countries under the topics listed in Passage 2.

Topics	Asian Countries	Western Countries
(1) Negotiating goal		
(2) Negotiating attitude		
(3) Personal style		
(4) Communication		
(5) Sensitivity to time		
(6) Emotionalism		
(7) Form of agreement		
(8) Building an agreement		
(9) Team organization		
(10) Risk taking		

2. Work in small groups. Compare your list of negotiating styles with your group members' and discuss: how crucial is a successful cross-cultural interaction for a Chinese businessman

when he is doing business with his counterparts from English-speaking countries.

3. Passage 2 listed "ten ways" that culture affects the style of negotiation. Choose one way in which there are cultural differences between China and the English-speaking countries. Study it further and then make a presentation to your class.

Advertising Styles

Advertising styles are defined by culture, as advertising reflects cultural values. This is one of the reasons why one single advertisement will rarely deliver similar responses. For effective international marketing and advertising it is necessary to understand a culture's influence. Cultural influences on product usage and people's attitudes can be analyzed for any product category or brand. A great deal of research on global advertising has examined how advertising in various countries or regions is similar to or differs from advertising in another country or region. Content analysis techniques have often compared specific executional appeals and design elements to determine whether the cultural differences between one specific country's advertising styles are unique. Cutitta, a global communications professional agency responsible for the flow of international advertising into information technology newspapers and magazines in 75 countries stated, "Cultural baggage is as relevant in cyberspace[①] as it is on paper and ink. The age-old question of 'how do I keep global advertising interesting without offending anyone?' does not go away." Thus, forgetting or ignoring the lessons learned over years by the mistakes and failures of multinational corporations' products and services and hundreds of research studies underscoring distinct cultural differences is foolish and ineffective. Cultural differences and adaptations to move closer to or not to offend consumers are as relevant to the environment that surrounds global interactive advertising as it has been to traditional forms of advertising.

Discussion

1. Work individually. List some Chinese trademarks that reflect Chinese culture. Then, in small groups, compare your list with your group members' and give your interpretations.

2. People from English-speaking countries don't like the following trademarks depicting animals. Discuss the possible reason(s) in small groups and then consult a dictionary to find out the answer.
"Goat"
"White Elephant"
"Dragon"

Classroom Tasks

Task 1

An advertising message encoded in one culture has to be decoded in another culture. Discuss possible distortions in the following cross-cultural miscommunication in commercials and then compare your answers in class.

(1) U. S. and British negotiators found themselves at a standstill when the American company proposed that they "table" particular key points. (Why are they at a standstill?)

(2) A U. S. napkin company advertised in Great Britain that "You could use no finer napkin at your dinner table." Sales were hardly brisk. (Why?)

(3) A golf ball manufacturing company packaged golf balls in packs of four for convenient purchase in Japan. Unfortunately items packaged in fours are unpopular. (Why?)

Task 2

The following are some well-known trademarks and the translations of some trademarks. Do some research on them individually, and then discuss their cultural implications in class.

同仁堂(药店)

三九胃泰(药)

稻香村(食品店)

四通 —— STONE (电脑)

Nike —— 耐克(运动鞋)

Marlboro——万宝路(香烟)

Task 3

1. Find a Chinese trademark or an advertisement which you think cannot be understood thoroughly without viewers (readers) knowing Chinese culture. Do some research on it and make a presentation to your class.

2. Find an English translation of a Chinese trademark or an advertisement (or you can translate one by yourself) that you think is closely linked to the target culture. You can carry out a survey of the translation among foreigners and find out what implication it presents to them. Make a presentation to class.

One example might be an advertisement of Mitsubishi (日本三菱汽车公司) for the American market: "Not all cars are created equal." The advertising message is based on the sentence "All men are created equal" taken from the Declaration of Independence of America and reveals a close connection to American history and politics.

Notes

① Passage 1 is extracted from "What is Cross-Culture" on http://www.crossculture.com.
Passage 2 is extracted from Salacuse, J. W., "The Top Ten Ways Culture Affected Negotiating Style" on http://fletcher.tufts.edu.
Passage 3 is extracted from Robert, M. S. & Ko, H., "Global Interactive Advertising: Defining What We Mean and Using What We Have Learned," http://www.jiad.org.
References for Classroom Tasks: Lanier, A. R., 1981, *Living in the U. S. A*, Chicago: Intercultural Press Inc. 王逢鑫,1997,"中国品牌命名的文化含义",《语文研究群言集》,广州:中山大学出版社。谢建平,"试论民族心理与商标语言创意",《外语与外语教学》,2001年第12期。彭石玉,"汉字商标词的跨文化传统",《外语与外语教学》,2001年第4期。

② Smith M. O. & J. F. Steward, "Communication for a Global Economics," in *Business Education Forum*, 49 April, 1995.

③ NAFTA: North Atlantic Free Trade Area,北大西洋自由贸易区。

④ GATT: General Agreement on Tariff and Trade,关税及贸易总协定。

⑤ ASEAN: Association of Southeast Asian Nations,东南亚国家联盟。

⑥ John Wayne:约翰·威恩(1907—1979),好莱坞西部牛仔影星;一人法则推崇者。

⑦ Cyberspace:在网络上交流的虚拟环境。

休闲与体育

　　西方人大多爱好体育运动。不同的民族对体育运动的不同偏爱也反映其不同的传统和价值观。譬如：美国人非常喜爱美式橄榄球、篮球和棒球运动。美国人通常认为，在这种有组织的集体运动项目中，运动员不分种族、经济地位、社会背景都能获得均等的获胜机会，并且能培养年轻人的拼搏、竞争精神，同时也是实现"美国梦"(from rags to riches)的典范。英国人除了喜欢足球、板球、橄榄球以外还喜欢被称之为"皇家运动"的赛马运动，这与英国的历史文化分不开。在我国，许多中老年人喜爱太极拳、气功等健身项目，因为人们认为这些运动具有平衡阴阳、消除紧张情绪等功效，这也充分体现了平衡、和谐的中国文化价值取向特征。

　　节假日，特别是传统节日，大多是民族历史和文化的结晶。节庆中各种活动负载着许多历史和文化内涵。因此，节假日是休闲活动，也是文化活动。了解一个民族或国家的休闲和体育活动方式是了解其文化特征的最直观、最生动的方法。本单元旨在引导学习者了解英美国家的节假日、休闲方式和体育活动，并对在这些方面折射出来的中西方不同的价值取向进行讨论。

Unit 8 ①

Leisure and Sports

Culture and leisure have much in common. Many activities are both cultural and leisure activities.

Reading and Discussion

How People Relax in the UK

Typical popular pastimes in the UK include listening to pop music, going to pubs, playing and watching sport, going on holidays, doing outdoor activities, and watching TV. The number of people playing sports has risen, partly due to the availability of more sporting facilities such as local leisure centres. As more people become aware of the necessity for exercise, it is estimated that one third of the adult population regularly takes part in outdoor sport and about a quarter in indoor sport.

Multi-screen cinemas have become more common and the number of people going to the cinema increased in the mid-1980s, which had fallen by more than half between 1971 and 1984. This was despite a large increase in the popularity of home videos: Britain has one of the highest rates of home video ownership in the world.

Pubs are an important part of British social life and more money is spent on drinking than on any other form of leisure activities. In a recent survey seven out of ten adults said they went to pubs, one third of them once a week or more often.

Holidays are the next major leisure cost, followed by television, radio, musical instruments, and eating out. If they have enough money, people travel more and take more holidays. The number going abroad increased from 7 million in the early 1970s to 17 million in the mid-80s, with Spain still the most popular foreign destination.

Despite the increase in TV watching, reading is still an important leisure activity in Britain and there is a very large number of magazines and books published on a wide variety of subjects. The biggest-selling magazines in Britain (after the TV guides) are women's and pop music publications. The best-selling books are not great works of literature but stories of mystery and romantic which sell in huge quantities. It has been estimated that only about 3 per cent of the population read "classics" such as Charles Dickens or Jane Austen, whereas the figures for popular book sales can be enormous, particularly if the books are connected with TV shows or dramatizations.

Discussion

1. In a small group, discuss how Chinese people spend their spare time in general. Then as a class, work out a list of typical pastimes in China with each group contributing one or two activities.

2. Tell your group members:

—What leisure activities do you prefer?

—How much time and money do you spend on them?
—Why are they enjoyable?
3. Discuss in groups:
— How many people in China do you think read "classics" nowadays?
— What sorts of books do Chinese people like reading most?
— What are your favorite sorts of books and magazines?
4. Discuss the questions in a small group and then report your discussion to the class.
— What are the main similarities and differences between Chinese and British pastimes?
— Are there any historical, cultural or social reasons that make them similar or different?

American Holidays

American holidays are influenced by American history, religion, and immigrants cultures. By studying American holidays, it is possible to understand American culture better. In the United States, there are federal (national) holidays, state holidays, and annual events. On federal holidays, federal and state offices, banks, schools, and companies close throughout the United States. Most people have a day off. There are ten federal holidays now. State holidays are legal holidays in a particular state or states. State offices, banks, schools, and companies in that state close. For annual events, offices and stores do not close, and people work as usual.

Easter, which falls on a spring Sunday that varies from year to year, celebrates the Christian belief in the resurrection of Jesus Christ. For Christians, Easter is a day of religious services and the gathering of family. Many Americans follow old traditions of coloring hard-boiled eggs and giving children baskets of candy.

Christmas Day, December 25, is another Christian holiday; it marks the birth of the Christ Child. Decorating houses and yards with lights, putting up Christmas trees, giving gifts, and sending greeting cards have become traditions even for many non-Christian Americans.

New Year's Day, of course, is January 1. The celebration of this holiday begins the night before, when Americans gather to wish each other a happy and prosperous coming year.

Thanksgiving Day is the fourth Thursday in November, but many Americans take a day of vacation on the following Friday to make a four-day weekend, during which they may travel long distances to visit family and friends. The holiday dates back to 1621, the year after the Puritans arrived in Massachusetts, determined to practice their dissenting religion without interference. After a rough winter, in which about half of them died, they turned for help to neighboring Indians, who taught them how to plant corn and other crops. The next fall's bountiful harvest inspired the Pilgrims to give thanks by holding a feast. The Thanksgiving feast became a national tradition—not only because so many other Americans have found prosperity but also because the Pilgrims' sacrifices for their freedom still captivate the imagination. To this day, Thanksgiving dinner almost always includes some of the foods served at the first feast: roast turkey, cranberry sauce, potatoes, pumpkin pie. Before the meal begins, families or friends usually pause to give thanks for their blessings, including the joy of being united for the occasion.

The Fourth of July, or *Independence Day*, honors the

nation's birthday—the signing of the Declaration of Independence on July 4, 1776. It is a day of picnics and patriotic parades, a night of concerts and fireworks. The flying of the American flag (which also occurs on Memorial Day and other holidays) is widespread. On July 4, 1976, the 200th anniversary of the Declaration of Independence was marked by grand festivals across the nation.

Martin Luther King Day: The Rev. Martin Luther King, Jr. , an African-American clergyman, is considered a great American because of his tireless efforts to win civil rights for all people through nonviolent means. Since his assassination in 1968, memorial services have marked his birthday on January 15. In 1986, that day was replaced by the third Monday of January, which was declared a national holiday.

Presidents' Day: Until the mid-1970s, February 22, birthday of George Washington, hero of the Revolutionary War and first president of the United States, was a national holiday. In addition, February 12, birthday of Abraham Lincoln, the president during the Civil War, was a holiday in most states. The two days have been joined, and the holiday has been expanded to embrace all past presidents. It is celebrated on the third Monday in February.

*Memorial Day*②: Celebrated on the fourth Monday of May, this holiday honors the dead. Although it originated in the aftermath of the Civil War, it has become a day on which the dead of all wars, and the dead generally, are remembered in special programs held in cemeteries, churches, and other public meeting places.

Labor Day: The first Monday of September, this holiday honors the nation's working people, typically with parades. For most Americans it marks the end of the summer vacation season, and for many students the opening of the school year.

*Columbus Day*③: On October 12, 1492, Italian navigator

Christopher Columbus landed in the New World. Although most other nations of the Americas observe this holiday on October 12, in the United States it takes place on the second Monday in October.

*Veterans Day*④: Originally called Armistice Day, this holiday was established to honor Americans who had served in World War I. It falls on November 11, the day when that war ended in 1918, but it now honors veterans of all wars in which the United States has fought. Veterans' organizations hold parades, and the president customarily places a wreath on the Tomb of the Unknown Soldier at Arlington *National Cemetery*⑤, across the Potomac River in Washington, D.C.

While not holidays, two other days of the year inspire colorful celebrations in the United States. On February 14, *Valentine's Day*, (named after an early Christian martyr), Americans give presents, usually candy or flowers, to the ones they love. On October 31, *Halloween* (the evening before *All Saints* or *All Hallows Day*), American children dress up in funny or scary costumes and go "trick or treating": knocking on doors in their neighborhood. The neighbors are expected to respond by giving them small gifts of candy or money. Adults may also dress in costume for Halloween parties.

Various ethnic groups in America celebrate days with special meaning to them even though these are not national holidays, such as the Chinese New Year.

Discussion

1. Many American holidays have legends behind them. Find more information about the legends and the history associated with one or two red-letter days in America described in Passage 2 and

talk about it in your group.

2. In a small group talk about Chinese festivals and holidays, their legends, history, religion, tradition or celebration. Then as a group, choose one Chinese festival, do some research into it, hold an extended discussion and make a presentation to the class.

Passage 3

Sports in Britain

The British have always been a nation of sport lovers and interest in all types of sport is as great today as it has ever been. Many sports which nowadays are played all over the world grew up to their present-day form in Britain. Football is perhaps the best example, but among the others are horse racing, golf, lawn tennis and rowing.

Association football ("soccer") is the most popular sport in Britain. It is played in most of the schools, and there are thousands of amateur teams for young men all over the country. But for most of the public, football is a professionals' game to be watched on Saturday afternoons at the local stadium.

Rugby football is more popular than association football in certain regions, and is the traditional game of most "public schools." It is played with an oval ball which is carried rather than kicked, and players try to stop the man with the ball by throwing him bodily to the ground. "Tries"⑥ are scored by carrying the ball over any part of the opponents' goal-line. Goals are scored by kicking the ball over the crossbar of a tall, H-shaped goal. In the commonest type of game there are fifteen players in each team.

People all over the world regard cricket as the most English of games. Its comparative slowness and quietness linked with its gentlemanly sportsmanship seem to reflect the English character. Yet even in England it is not nearly as popular as football. In fact in recent years it has become less popular than before. On the other hand, the annual "test matches"① between England and other Commonwealth countries, especially Australia, inspire considerable public excitement.

The game which both men and women are most likely to play after leaving school is *tennis*. Some join a tennis club, but most find a partner and go to one of the thousands of public tennis courts which can be hired by the hour. In tennis, as in other cases, the amateur sport has given way irresistibly to professionalism, and the best tennis players in the world are those who make it their livelihood.

While the young are playing tennis on the public tennis courts, the old—women as well as men—may be playing bowls on the public bowling-green nearby. A bowling-green is a beautifully smooth lawn. At one end is placed a white ball, about the size of a tennis ball. From the other end a group of players take it in turns to roll along the grass a large, heavy wooden ball so that it stops as near the white ball as possible. It is a peaceful game, yet one demanding considerable judgment, since the bowls are weighed so as to roll in a slight curve.

Another outdoor game which many men and women of all ages become passionately fond of is *golf*. This is played over an area of countryside containing eighteen small holes, each indicated by a flag, and each one several hundreds of yards away from the next. Each player (there are usually two playing against each other) has a small white ball which he has to hit towards and into each hole in turn, counting the number of strokes he takes. There is no time limit. The winner is the one who completes the course in the smallest number of strokes.

An annual race which is universally popular is the boat race between Oxford and Cambridge Universities. This takes place on a stretch of the River Thames. It gives rise to weeks of nation-wide comment and discussion every year.

One reason for the great interest in sport in Britain is the English-man's fondness for a little "flutter" (a slang expression for a bet or gamble). Gambling has always been an integral part of such sports as horse-racing and dog-racing and, in recent times, doing the "football pools" has become a national pastime.

Horse-racing is chiefly a betting sport, and is studied eagerly by many people who seldom see a horse. The horses are owned and trained by a few rich people, and usually ridden by professional jockeys.

Football "pools" in which bets are made on results of matches, provide amusement for millions of people, both men and women. "Filling in the pools," i. e. forecasting wins, losses and draws on a printed form, takes place during the week; then on Saturdays, all these millions of people listen to their radio or television set to check their forecasts. Anyone who gets them all right will win a very large sum of money.

Whether as gambler, spectator or player, most Englishmen have some interest in at least some sports.

Discussion

1. In a small group discuss:

Of the sports mentioned which ones are your favourites? Describe one of them in detail to your group members.

2. Discuss in your group:

— What are the most popular sports in China nowadays?

— What are the popular sports practiced at Chinese schools?
— What sports are unique to China?
— What sports do Chinese people play for gambling?
— Do you gamble?
— Do you think gambling is a harmless activity?

The Meanings of Football in the United States

America has developed some spectator sports® of its own which are little practiced elsewhere, in particular American football and baseball. Football is derived from the English game of rugby, which has been adopted in other English-speaking countries but only in a few parts of Europe (notably in southwestern France). The American form requires very sophisticated equipment and considerable organization. It is a game which cannot easily be adapted to an empty patch of ground where boys use coats for a goal. It is played at school, but by its nature it tends to attract a rather restricted group of boys, and normally played by those who hope to become serious players. Apart from the university teams there are many professional football teams, and they play in large stadia on Saturday afternoons, often before large crowds. The game is played with an oval ball; players may carry it and tackle each other (so that one player may throw another down as part of the game). The rules are complicated, and the game in inherently dangerous. Many players have been seriously injured or even killed in the past, but in order to avoid such injuries the most elaborate protective clothing has been developed. With dramatic protection for his head, shoulders and chest, and a visor over his face, a player when fully equipped looks like a ferocious and malevolent visitor from another planet. The average football player looks formidable enough in private life, with his close-cropped hair and well-trained toughness, but a team of these armored giants looks frightening indeed.

Football in the United States displays themes particularly important in the society: sexuality, technological complexity, coordination, and specialization, as well as the tendency to violence, although that violence is expressed within the framework of teamwork, specialization, and mechanization. In this view, "The football team looks very much like a small scale model of the American corporation: compartmentalized, highly sophisticated in the coordinated application of a differentiated, specialized technology, turning out a winning product in a competitive market." (Montague and Morais 1976: 39) Thus, the football game is a model of the most important productive unit in the United States: the business firm. By watching football, Americans are watching a model of the way their own world works. Because football is a small-scale model of that world, it allows us to understand it. It "renders visible and directly comprehensible a system that is far too large and complex to be directly comprehended by any individual." How many of us can understand the interconnections among all aspects of the American economic system?

Beyond this, however, football is a model of the traditional route to success in the United States. Dedication, hard work, and self-sacrifice for the good of others (here, the football team) are held up as the basic principles on which success is based and are the characteristics most praised in individual players. Football is the staging of a real event in which the principles of success are shown to work. The success model is also illustrated in football commentary. The accomplishments of each player are compared with those of others, and the rewards of the system—money and recognition—are extended to the players on the basis of their performances. To the extent that football is a model of the real world, the audience sees the actors being evaluated according to objective criteria and rewarded according to performance. This process is at the ideological core of the traditional culture of the United States and is ultimately related to the productive process in the society.

Discussion

1. Work in groups. Comment on the following opinions connected with American football. Do you agree with the author of Passage 4?

— The football team looks like a small-scale model of the American corporation.

— Football helps one to understand the American economic system.

— By watching football, Americans are watching a model of the way their own world works.

— Football is a model of the traditional route to success in the US.

— Football shows how the principles of success work.

2. This passage suggests that sports help integrate society by revealing its social structure and embodying cultural themes. Based on the idea, comment on other sports (like Chinese Chess, Qigong, Tai Chi, Sword Dances in China or baseball in America and cricket in Australia) in groups.

Classroom Tasks

Task 1

The following are the views about the significance of winning expressed by some American prominent coaches. Read them and discuss the questions in groups.

"*Winning is not everything; it is the only thing.*"

"*Every time you win, you're reborn; when you lose, you die a little.*"

"*No one ever learns anything by losing.*"

"*Defeat is worse than death because you have to live with defeat.*"

1. Discussion questions:

— Do you agree with the views?

— What are your views about the importance of winning?

— If you were a football coach, what would be your motto?

2. Compare the views of American coaches with Chinese values of winning in sports in general.

Task 2

Americans look to their sporting heroes to be models of courage, discipline, strong character, and success. No full understanding of America is possible without an understanding of its sports idols. Here is a short passage about the American hero, Michael Jordan. Read it and discuss the questions in groups.

America has adopted Michael Jordan as its hero of the 1990s. Michael Jordan is an American icon in a multitude of ways, but above all he speaks as a cultural icon with his amazing, all-around, graceful, improvisational and lightning quick skills on the basketball court. It is Jordan's basketball skill above all that characterizes him as not only a black hero, taking the street game to the NBA, but as a truly American hero. It is his style that has captivated American audiences and audiences around the world for more than a decade. Jordan has taken his game far beyond the original white American game of basketball. Jordan's game has effectively reinvented basketball with his own black cultural style. Michael Jordan has captured the hearts and minds of black and white America as a basketball player who symbolizes the American Dream and has become a true American icon. With his distinctive style of play, he has dominated the NBA since his rookie year and been deemed the greatest basketball player of all time by publications and broadcasts. He has truly become the new American hero, the black American hero that the nation has needed to unify its divided population.

1. Discussion questions:

— What have you learned about Michael Jordan from the passage above?

— What do you know about the American Dream?

— Why do you think Michael Jordan is said to symbolize the American Dream?

2. Describe a Chinese sport figure who you think is an icon.

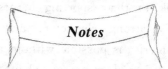

Notes

① Passage 1 is extracted from Harvey, P. & R. Jones, 1992, *Britain Explored*, London: Longman, pp. 130,131,134,136.

Passage 2 is extracted from http://usinfo.state.gov.

Passage 3 is extracted from Tregidgo, P. S., 1978, *A Background to English*, London: Longman, pp. 59—61.

Passage 4 is adapted from Lanier, A. R., 1981, *Living in the U. S. A*, Chicago: Intercultural Press Inc, pp. 187—188 and Nanda, S. and R. L. Warms, 1998, *Cultural Anthropology*

6th ed,Washington:Wadsworth Publishing Company, pp. 308—309.

The passage in Task 2 is extracted from http://www.findarticles.com.

② Memorial Day:阵亡将士纪念日。
③ Columbus Day:哥伦布纪念日。
④ Veterans Day:退伍军人节。
⑤ Arlington National Cemetery:阿灵顿国家公墓。
⑥ tries:(橄榄球)持球触地得分。
⑦ test matches:锦标赛。
⑧ spectator sports:能吸引观众的运动。

食品与保健

　　食物是人类最基本的生物需求。而人类的生存条件、地理环境、社会发展常常决定其所享用的食品,食品同时也折射出一个民族的传统和文化。譬如:典型的中餐一般由饭和菜组成,而菜一般有荤有素,菜的数量通常是双数,这些都反映了中国人追求平衡、和谐的理念。"麦当劳"可以说代表着美国的快餐文化,其机械的烹饪程序、高度统一的标准、快速方便的服务,反映了20世纪20年代以来美国社会高速发展的经济和快节奏的生活方式。

　　同样,不同的文化对疾病的解释、预防、治疗,以及对待疼痛,甚至死亡均有不同的理解和信念。这种现象在中西医学界表现得尤为突出。中国的医学以阴阳为根本原则,认为阴阳失调人就会生病。在治疗疾病方面更注重预防以及对病人全身心阴阳平衡的综合调养。而西医更强调"头疼医头,脚疼医脚"。本单元旨在引导学习者对在食物和医学保健方面所折射出的文化因素进行讨论,深入探讨中国医学中反映出来的深层文化。

Unit 9 [1]

Food and Healthcare

Food is a basic biological need, a fundamental ingredient for the survival of a group. The environment often determines what sorts of foods are available and also influences which foods are culturally preferred and which are prohibited.

Jill Dubisch[2]

Reading and Discussion

Fast Food and American Culture

The rise of the fast food restaurant would not have been possible without concomitant changes in American culture. Beginning in the 1920s, thanks largely to developments in technology and industry, the American lifestyle began to change. Formerly distinctive regional and ethnic cultures were now meeting up with each other, blurring differences in identity. More people were moving off the farm and into the city in search of lucrative and exciting careers. In addition, the widespread use of inventions like the telephone and the increasing acceptance of mass media meant that there was a larger degree of cultural interaction.

The development of an affordable automobile and the simultaneous governmental support of new road systems physically reinforced this cultural melding, enabling car owners, especially, to go to places they had never been before. This sparked a boom in the tourist industry: travelers who once went by rail, boat, or horse, were now moving faster by car, and began to value things such as speed and convenience as part of their trips. Not only did they need affordable and reliable places to stay, but they also needed similarly reliable places to eat.

While local diners and eateries offered good, wholesome home-cooked meals, they were often located far away from main thoroughfares, making them inconvenient for the interstate traveler. Travelers, however, were not the only ones eating on the run; private dining, once a formal ritual among family members and close friends, was becoming a thing of the past, and eating in public was becoming much more acceptable for everyone. The increased pace of life, especially in urban areas, meant that people no longer ate as a group around the table, but favored sandwiches and other foods that could be eaten quickly and on the go. Food was becoming merely a fuel, like gasoline, for the human working machines.

McDonald's, the most successful fast food franchise, was started in 1955 by Ray A. Kroc (1902—1984), a Chicago milk shake machine salesman. Kroc's success lay in his approach not specifically to cooking individual food items, but in conceiving of his franchise operation in its entirety. His outlets were food factories—everything was systematized to ensure sameness, even the smiles on the clerks' faces. Kroc did not promise the best burger in the world, but the same burger throughout the world; indeed, the public came to accept this dictum, preferring predictability over quality. Every McDonald's had the same menu and the same general layout (with minor variations to acknowledge regional differences). The workers, all dressed alike, used the same techniques and equipment to prepare the food in the same way. In addition, Kroc established these as "family" restaurants that were clean, well-lit, and free from pay phones and pin ball machines that would encourage loitering.

The 1960s through the 1990s was considered the "golden age" of fast food, and saw the explosion of various fast food chains and the subsequent creation of "the strip"③ in almost every town—the piece of road or highway flanked by franchise after franchise—which became a trademark feature of the suburban landscape. Fast food restaurants along the strip sold not only hamburgers, but also hotdogs, fish, pizza, ice cream, chicken, and roast beef sandwiches.

Franchise success was almost wholly based on the principles of standardization and a machine ethic. This included the laborers working within, who were treated as parts of the machine meant to run as efficiently as possible. Training was based on the idea that basic skills substituted for high turn-over rates—the guarantee that the food could still be made the same even from unskilled hands. The short order cook of the early diners, who was considered an artisan of sorts, was replaced by teenager working for minimum wage and no benefits.

Critics coined the pejorative phrase "fast food culture" as a metaphor for the quick-service industries and excessive standardization seen in late-twentieth-century culture and consumption. This homogenization, they believed, not only affected American culture, erasing once vibrant ethnic and regional traditions, but also was beginning to influence the entire world—a cultural imperialism enacted on an international level.

By the final decades of the twentieth century, Americans had fully embraced their "fast food culture." In 1994 alone, fast food restaurants in the United States sold over 5 billion hamburgers, making it a favorite meal and an important commodity. In 1996, seven percent of the population ate at the 11,400 McDonald's each day; males from their mid-teens to their early 30s comprised 75 percent of this business. By this time, fast food had become a cultural phenomenon that reached beyond America's borders. In 1996 McDonald's owned over 7,000 restaurants in other countries, including: 1,482 in Japan; 430 in France; 63 in China; two each in Bulgaria and Andorra; and one in Croatia. These outlets acknowledged some cultural differences—in Germany they sold beer, in France they sold wine, and in Saudi Arabia they had separate sections for men and women and closed four times a day for prayers. But for the most part the fast food fare was the same, homogenizing culture on an international level.

Discussion

1. List the changes in American society and culture that helped develop American fast food by finishing the following chart. Then compare the information in your chart with your partner's.

Developments in Technology and Industry	Changes in Lifestyle
Use of telephone;	Moving off the farm to the city;

Unit 9

2. In small groups, illustrate the following ideas drawn from Passage 1 with examples.

— Food was becoming merely a fuel for the human working machines.

— Franchise success was almost wholly based on the principles of standardization and a machine ethic.

— "Fast food culture" was coined as a metaphor for the quick-service industries and excessive standardization in late-twentieth-century culture and consumption.

— Fast food has become a cultural phenomenon.

3. In small groups, describe the features in McDonald's. Are the features the same as what you see in their franchises in China? Describe in brief any other foreign fast food franchises in China. Discuss which group(s) of Chinese people (children, young, adults, old) accept foreign fast food more easily? Why?

4. Comment on the cultural differences in McDonald's franchises in different countries.

Passage 2

Food and Perception

China has the oldest continuing culture of any nation in the world. About 500 B. C., the philosophies of Confucianism and Taoism became the prime motivating forces in the development of the cuisine. The counterbalance of these two major philosophies became the basis of Chinese cuisine as an art.

Confucius encouraged a sense of balance and harmony. For example, when meats were used as ingredients, they could not overpower the rice included in the same meal. He also emphasized the aesthetic aspects of cooking and eating. He said a proper dish should appeal to the eye as well as to the palate. For example, intricately carved vegetables are a common decoration.

The distinctive process of preparing Chinese cuisine is based on Confucius and his philosophy of balance. There is a division between *fan*, Chinese for grains and other starch foods, and *chai*, vegetables and meat dishes. A balanced meal, then, must have an appropriate amount of *fan* and *chai*.

The main principle of Tao is a life in perfect accord with nature. The basic assumption of Taoism is that there is an underlying pattern of direction of the universe that cannot be explained verbally or intellectually. The Tao is this underlying pattern, commonly known as the *Way*. The Taoist ideal is a person who leads a simple, spontaneous, and meditative life close to nature. Taoists were encouraged to explore roots, fungi, herbs, marine vegetation, and other natural foods to discover their life-giving elements.

There is also a belief in a balance that governs all of life and nature—the *yin* and *yang*. Originally, *yang* meant the sunny side of a hill and *yin* the shady side. *Yang* is the bright, dry, warm aspect of the cosmos. Males have more *yang* quality. *Yin* is the dark, moist, cool aspect. Female have more *yin* quality.

Foods also have *yin* and *yang* qualities. Oily and fried foods, pepper-hot flavoring, fatty meat, and oil-rich plant food like peanuts are "heaty" *yang* foods. Most water plants, crustaceans, and certain beans are cooling *yin* foods.

Remember, all elements of a culture interrelate. Half of China is mountainous or unsuitable for cultivation. China cannot depend on large animals like cattle that are land intensive. Through necessity, the Chinese have used all forms of edible ingredients—from lotus roots, birds' nests, and sea cucumbers to pig brains and fish lips.

Because of a scarcity of fuel and raw materials, stir-frying was developed. Small pieces of meat, poultry, fish, or vegetables take only a few minutes to cook and thus save fuel.

For at least 5,000 years, rice has been grown in China. Its importance has made it synonymous with food and life. Rice is the symbol of well-being and fertility. Leaving one's job is called breaking one's rice bowl. It is considered bad luck to upset a rice bowl. And the worst of all insults is to take another's bowl of rice and empty it onto the ground.

Discussion

1. Do you agree with the following ideas? Give facts to support your opinion.

— The balance in Chinese cuisine: starch foods and dishes; *yin* and *yang* in cuisine.

— Taoists were encouraged to explore natural foods to discover their life-giving elements.

— Due to the lack of suitable land for cultivation, the Chinese have used all forms of edible ingredients.

— Because of a scarcity of fuel and raw materials, stir-frying was developed.

— Rice is the symbol of well-being and fertility.

2. Culture defines what is appropriate to eat and at the same time, what you eat may define your membership in a culture or subculture. What a family eats for breakfast or lunch often reflects its ethnic background or geographic location.

Individually, do either of the following tasks.

— Read menus from Western restaurants in your living place or in books and compare them with menus from Chinese restaurants. Present what they tell about the cultures to your class.

— Do some reading and research on Chinese cuisine in a certain area, such as in your hometown, and then give a presentation of culture and food there to your class.

Culturally Competent in Healthcare

Culture influences an individual's health beliefs, behaviors, activities and medical treatment outcomes. Because of the significant influence of culture upon health and related outcomes, health care professionals should be culturally competent in order to provide optimum health care to patients.

The most intimate relationship

Dealing with people's health means dealing with them at the most personal level. Beliefs about disease, pain, and death need to be considered. Indeed, in some cultures, seeking medical care represents the last resort after a long and painful struggle; for others, the slightest discomfort spurs a visit to the clinic. Some cultures, such as the Hmong①, believe that the body and soul are intricately connected and illness is a signal that the soul is "wandering." For some people, death might be the ultimate reward; for others it represents a dreaded judgment. And, of course, delivering bad news is difficult, regardless of cultural norms. In some cultures, however, a poor prognosis is never shared with the patient.

Cultural competency means considering many options and being more careful about making judgments. For example, scars and bruises that suggest abuse in Western culture could actually be symbols of accepted healing methods or sacred rituals. In addition, different parts of the body are considered sacred in different cultures.

The challenges for competency

Cultural competency in healthcare holds four major challenges for providers. The first is the straightforward challenge of recognizing clinical differences among people of different ethnic and racial groups (e.g. higher risk of hypertension in African Americans and of diabetes in certain Native American groups).

The second, and far more complicated, challenge is communication. This deals with everything from the need for interpreters to nuances of words in various languages. Many patients, even in Western cultures, are reluctant to talk about personal matters such as sexual activity or chemical use. How do we overcome this challenge among more restricted cultures?

The third challenge is ethics. While Western medicine is among the best in the world, we do not have all the answers. Respect for the belief systems of others and the effects of those beliefs on well-being are critically important to competent care.

The final challenge involves trust. For some patients, authority figures are immediately mistrusted, sometimes for good reason. Having seen or been victims of atrocities at the hands of authorities in their homelands, many people are as wary of caregivers themselves as they are of the care.

Time for change

To provide the best care for our changing patient base, we need to make important changes in our daily interactions with many patients and, on a more basic level, in our training of physicians. We need to give ourselves a large dose of "cultural humility," so we can be more comfortable in seeking information about the cultures we serve. We need to learn to ask questions sensitively and show respect for different beliefs. And we need to try to understand all of our patients and the care they seek.

Most important, we must listen to our patients carefully. The main source of problems in caring for diverse patient groups is lack of understanding and tolerance. Too often, neither the doctor nor the patient understands the other's perspective.

Gaining and fine-tuning sensitivity in these areas can be a highly satisfying experience, both professionally and personally. If we view the challenges of cultural diversity as an opportunity rather than as yet another problem, the rewards might just be as rich and varied as the patients we now are fortunate enough to see.

Discussion

1. In a small group discuss the following questions:
— When you are ill, what do you usually think is the cause of illness?
— What's your attitude towards death?
— Do Chinese people usually share a poor prognosis with the patient?

2. In groups of three or four, illustrate the four major challenges for cultural competency in healthcare with example:
— recognizing clinical differences among different ethnic groups (e. g. stomach problems in Chinese);
— intercultural communication (e. g. language barriers, nonverbal messages and formality and politeness);
— ethics (e. g. What are the chief problems your sickness has caused for you? What kind of treatment do you think you should receive for your sickness? What do you fear most about your sickness?);

— trust (e. g. At whose hands will you submit to an operation?).

3. In a small group, discuss differences between Western medicine and traditional Chinese medicine in beliefs, the explanation, treatment, and prevention of illness.

4. Make a survey on those people who have had medical treatment in a different culture (country) such as a Chinese in another country or a foreigner in China. Have they encountered any misunderstandings or problems in the different healthcare background. Share the result of your survey with your group members and discuss cultural implications underlying the misunderstandings or problems.

Passage 4

Fundamental Asian Health Concepts

Yin and *yang*. All Asian groups define health as the harmonious balance between the forces of *yin* and *yang* and the corresponding conditions of hot and cold. Illness is attributed to an upset of this balance. Illness can be cured only if the balance is restored by lowering the excessive trait or increasing the deficient one. Most traditional medical investigation involves a search for imbalances within the patient's physical and mental self. Treatment focuses on the restoration of balance.

Hot and cold theory of disease. Everything in the universe is classified as either *yin*, which is "cold," or *yang*, which is "hot." The terms refer not to temperatures but to attributes and/or conditions based upon *yin* and *yang*. The hot/cold classification, which is applied as much to recently discovered diseases and biomedical treatments as to traditional ones, includes parts of the body and their functions (e. g., childbirth), diseases, foods, and medicines. A "hot" disease is treated by a "cold" medicine in order to rebalance the patient's condition. Linden tea, for example, which may be served hot, is considered a "cold" herb and is used to treat "hot" ailments. Penicillin, on the other hand, is considered a "hot" treatment because it can produce diarrhea and rashes, which are viewed as "hot" symptoms.

While not all Asian patients subscribe to these beliefs, no caregiver can afford to ignore the possibility that a particular patient may consciously or unconsciously be influenced by them to some degree. Their effect on both trust and adherence to prescribed treatments can be enormous. For example, water and fruit juice are "cold" substances that are to be avoided during illness and after childbirth, times that produce a "cold" condition. Consequently, Asian patients may greatly curtail their fluid intake and may be reluctant to bathe or shower for as long as 30 days, since water conducts "cold" into the body. If a Western-trained physician prescribes cold liquids to a person with a cold who is running a high fever, not only might the patient ignore the physician's advice, but he or she might also question the medical knowledge of the physician.

Qi, or *Ch'i*. Other important Asian concepts about health care concern blood and an energy force known in Chinese as *Qi*, or *Ch'i*. The generation and flow of blood through the vessels, and the flow of the energy force (*Qi*) through the meridians or acupuncture points, are the fundamental factors most involved in the harmonious/disharmonious states of the body. Blood is believed to be "ruled by the heart, governed by the spleen, and stored in the liver." *Qi* involves all organs but has a special relationship with the liver, lungs, and spleen. When the flow of *Qi* is blocked by a broken bone or disease, acupuncture at the meridians permits the force to flow freely again.

Harmony. Diet plays a major role in Asian health and illness beliefs, and many preventives and cures depend on regulating or changing the diet. Because foods and beverages are classified as either *yin* or *yang*, "hot" or "cold," what one eats has a major impact upon the balance and harmony essential to health. Many Asian groups, such as the Chinese, Japanese, and Koreans, believe that their cuisine naturally balances these forces. To some extent, this may be true. For example, a study of the symptoms of menopause among women in rural Japan and women in the West found fewer menopausal symptoms among the Japanese women, a finding attributed to a Japanese diet high in soybean, a substance that contains natural estrogen.

In general, most Asians do not seem to perceive any great dichotomy between the Eastern and Western medical belief systems. There is a widespread belief that some illnesses are best treated by traditional Chinese medicine and others by Western physicians. For example, Western physicians are often consulted for problems involving dentistry, fever, allergy, eye problems, heart attack, stroke, surgery, diabetes, and cancer, while traditional physicians and herbalists are sought for asthma, arthritis, bruises, sprains, lumbago, stomach problems, and hypertension.

Often a Western physician is visited for diagnosis and treatment, but, once the complaint has been diagnosed, the person will self-medicate by using herbs and patent medicines purchased over the counter. If the Western treatment doesn't bring immediate relief of the symptoms, the patient may seek the care of a traditional physician or healer. The same thing may happen if a Western diagnosis is rejected because it bears a negative prognosis (including diagnosis of a long-term illness or of an illness that cannot be fully cured) or because surgery is advised. The traditional treatment may either replace the Western treatment or be used along with it. Many Asian patients do not disclose the use of traditional care and medications to their Western physicians because the two medical domains—Western and traditional medicine—are seen as entirely separate. Some patients may also fear that the Western physician (an authority figure) will disapprove, or they believe that disclosure of the traditional care would violate the relationship of trust.

Discussion

1. Discuss in groups:

— What do you know about "*yin* and *yang*," "hot and cold" theories in medical treatments?

— Do you know any explanation of the theories in disease and medical treatments?

— Do you know any other medical treatments especially in Chinese traditional medicine?

2. Generally speaking, which medical system do you think Chinese people trust more: a Western medical system, a traditional Chinese medical system or would they rather ask for different treatment for different problems? What makes them have the belief?

Classroom Tasks

Task 1

The following passage is taken from "A Cross-Cultural Experience: A Chinese Anthropologist in the United States" by

Huang Shu-min, a professor at Iowa State University, who was born and raised in many areas of China. Read the passage and discuss the questions in groups.

One aspect of American culture that I have not been able to develop full appreciation of is food. Brought up in a culture whose menu contains a wide range of food varieties and flavors, I consider American food rather plain. And, worst of all when I have American meals, I often feel full rather quickly, sometimes after just the salad. But then in a short while, I will feel hungry.

Originally, I thought that this was a phenomenon particular to me, mainly because I do not have a taste for American food and hence cannot eat too much of it. Believing that Chinese dishes have a better taste than anything else, I never had the slightest idea that Americans could have the same problem when eating Chinese food.

One day, my wife and I invited a few colleagues of mine over for supper. Our conversation somehow had focused on food preparation in different cultures. I jokingly remarked that even though I am an anthropologist by training, my appetite does not really match my intellectual capacity. I told them of the peculiar problem I had in eating American meals and indicated the possible reason as I saw it. On hearing that, one of our guests burst into laughter. "This is exactly the same problem I have when I come to your house for dinner," he said. "Even though I am quite full now, I will be very hungry by the time I arrive home. And I used to think this was so because of the strange taste of Chinese food!" I was surprised to find that the same opinion was shared by others.

Questions:

1. What is the possible cause(s) of this cross-cultural problem? (You can compare differences in content and variety

between American and Chinese food such as staple food, meat, vegetables.)

2. Does the similar problem occur when you have meals in a different area? (e. g. people from the north of China having meals in the south of China)

3. What are cultural or subcultural implications underlying this digestive problem?

Task 2

Table manners, like a great many everyday events, are heavily laden with cultural meaning. They are part of an inventory of symbolic behaviors that may be encoded to communicate messages about oneself. Read the passage below on table manners and describe Chinese table manners in general. (e. g. What is the overriding rule of Chinese table customs?)

In general Westerners try to eat neatly, without making a lot of noise. If something on the table is out of their reach, they politely ask someone to pass it to them. Food should be lifted up to the mouth. Do not bend over to eat it. Sit up as straight as you can without being uncomfortable. Do not talk with your mouth full.

Table napkins are placed on your lap, folded in half if they are very large. If you are in a small group, it is polite to wait to start eating until the host sits down and begins. With larger groups, you may begin after noting that a few people have begun. You may also begin if the host urges you to.

Use your fork, knife and spoon to eat your food. There are some exceptions, like lobster and corn on the cob, cookies, shrimp, and fried chicken and other foods. Better watch what other people do. If you do eat with your hands, don't lick your fingers to clean them. Use the napkin carefully. If you have to take food out of your mouth, such as a pit or bone, do it carefully and quietly. It is not polite to pick your teeth at the table to remove trapped food. If you must do this before the end of the meal, excuse yourself and go to the restroom.

Task 3

It's been said that Americans are obsessed with food. This can be illustrated by the modern-day vocabulary. For examples: Getting close to someone is called "buttering them up"; drawing attention to yourself may be "hamming it up"; a cute woman is called a "hot tomato"; your boss is the "big cheese"; when you blush you can turn "beet red"; the things that are necessary for life are called "bread and butter", etc. Work in class:

— Think of more examples in the English language which are linked with food. (e. g. apple polisher)

— Think of similar examples in the Chinese language.

Task 4

A Chinese film entitled *Gua Sha* (《刮痧》) tells a story about a grandfather who practiced *gua sha*, an ancient treatment in traditional Chinese medicine on his grandson. This is misunderstood by American doctors, who then send the father of the son to court to be charged for abusing his own son. Eventually the child is taken from the family. The marks of the *gua sha* treatment have also led to investigations. See the film and discuss the implications underlying the conflict in medical treatments between Chinese and Western cultures.

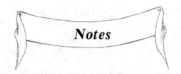

Notes

① Passage 1 is extracted from Woloson, W., "Fast Food" in Gale Encyclopedia of Popular Culture located at http://www.findarticles.com.

Passage 2 is extracted from Jandt, F. E., 1995, *International Communication: An Introduction*, California: Sage Publication Ltd, pp. 143—146.

Passage 3 is extracted from Peter A. S., 1998, "Culturally Competent Healthcare: Meeting the Challenges Can Improve Outcomes and Enrich Patient Care," MD Vol 103 / No 2 Feb, located at http://www.postgradmed.com.

Passage 4 is extracted from "Culture—Sensitive Health care: Asian," located at http://www.multicultural.vt.edu.

The passage of Task 1 is extracted from Huang Shu-min. "A Cross-Cultural Experience: A Chinese Anthropologist in the United States," Angeloni, E. (ed.), 1996, Annual Editions: Anthropology 96/97, Guilford: Dushkin Publishing Group/ Brown & Benchmark Publishers, p. 32.

The passage in Task 2 is extracted from "Table Manners" located at http://www.lifeintheusa.com.

② Dubisch, J., 1993, "You Are What You Eat: Religious Aspects of the Health Food Movement" in *Applying Cultural Anthropology: An Introductory Reader*, 2nd ed., California: Mayfield Publishing Company, p. 90.

③ "the strip": 市区或郊区商店、加油站、餐厅、酒吧密集的街道。

④ Hmong: 苗族, 苗人在 17—19 世纪中叶陆续由中国西南迁入越中、越老边境高山地区。语言属于汉藏语系苗瑶语族苗语支。

人际关系

　　由于地域环境、生活方式、宗教信仰、经济状况、年龄以及受教育程度等诸多方面的差异,来自不同民族与文化的人在处理人与人之间的关系时,在观念上和方式上也各异。譬如,对"朋友""友谊",不同的民族,不同的文化赋予其不同的含义。美国人的"朋友"概念较宽泛,"a friend"可能指一个亲密的伙伴,也可能只是一个同事或熟人。相对美国人而言,中国人则对"朋友"、"同事"、"熟人"有比较明确的区分。中西方文化对"朋友""友谊"的界定、理解与期望存在差异,相互间交流的方式也无不受到文化价值观的影响。在跨文化交际中,如果对此缺乏了解,就有可能在交流双方间产生费解或误解,甚至会无意中伤害对方,造成不必要的损失。本单元提供了阅读文章和课堂讨论,旨在引导学习者观察跨文化交际中的人际交往实例,从中西方文化的深层角度,对这些实例进行思考、分析和讨论,以提高在人际交往过程中的跨文化交际意识和能力。

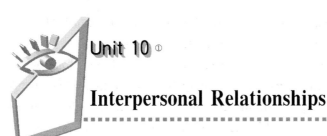

Unit 10 ①

Interpersonal Relationships

Interpersonal relations ... are not easy to characterize; they vary according to geographical location, life-style, ethnic background, religious orientation, socioeconomic level, age, and education level.

—*Kathy J. Irving*②

Part One Reading and Discussion

Friends

What is meant by the word "friend"? The dictionary defines it as: "one attached to another by affection or esteem." Americans use the word freely—that is, a friend may not be a person to whom there is a great attachment. A friend might be a casual acquaintance or an intimate companion. Friends may have known each other since childhood or they may have recently met. It is difficult to formulate a precise definition of this word as it is used in the United States, because it covers many types of relationships. "My friend and I went to the show last night," "My friends gave me the name of a good doctor." "My friend consoled me when I was depressed." We hear daily references to the word "friend" without knowing the quality of the friendship referred to.

It is common for Americans to have different "circles of friends" such as church friends, work friends, or sports friends. A person may choose not to involve members of different circles in the same activity. (One's friends from the office may never meet one's friends from the sports club.) Terms such as "office mate" and "tennis partner" indicate the segregation of friends. The office mate is a friend in the office and the tennis partner is a friend on the courts. People have different types of friends: one may have many good friends and one best friend. "Best friends" are usually two people of the same sex who have known each other for a long period of time. People usually have more casual friends than close or best friends.

Americans are geographically mobile and learn to develop friendships easily and quickly. Approximately one out of every five American families moves every year. People relocate because they begin new jobs, attend a distant college, get married, have children or simply want a change in their lives. Perhaps as a consequence of this, people form and end friendships quickly. Students attending two or three universities during their undergraduate and graduate years may change their circles of friends several times.

Relationships based on a common activity may fade or end when the activity ends. Students might meet in classes and remain friends for the duration of the course and then stop seeing each other after the final examination. The same holds true for neighbours who are the closest of friends until one moves away. In these relationships, shared daily experiences form the foundation for the relationship. Enduring friendships develop when individuals have similar interests and a common outlook on life. The high rate of mobility in the United States can explain a great deal about transient friendships.

It is easy to be misled by instant friendships which may appear to be deep and personal but are really superficial. Friendship and friendliness are not synonymous. Friendliness characterizes much of American daily interaction but is not always an indication of friendship. Strangers may share life histories without any intention of pursuing a relationship. Characterizing instant friendships is the appearance of two people becoming close but, in reality, there is no strong bond between them. Brief encounters do not always imply desire for further contact. Many people frequently smile or say, "Have a nice day" or "See ya later," or even extend an invitation as part of a cultural pattern of politeness. Such expressions do not suggest an offer of continued friendship.

Discussion

Discuss the questions in groups.

1. The first paragraph of Passage 1 tells us briefly what the word "friend" means to American people. What do you think the word "friend" means to Chinese people?

2. Do you have different circles of friends? Do you segregate your friends from different circles?

3. Do you agree that: " 'Best friends' are usually two people of the same sex who have known each other for a long period of time. People usually have more casual friends than close or best friends"?

4. Do you think it is generally true to say that Chinese people "form and end friendship quickly"?

5. Comment on the statements: "Friendship and friendliness are not synonymous." "A Westerner can be friendly without being

intimate while an Easterner tends to be intimate without being friendly."

Friendship

The question "What are the rights and obligations of friendship?" is a question that is usually not asked. Like many other aspects of our social life, friendship is taken for granted. How to relate, to interact with friends, is not something we consciously learn, it is something we do without asking how or why. It's natural, we feel, and international. Everyone has friends and so naturally everyone behaves the same way towards them. While the former is obviously true, the latter is not, and it is from often subtle differences in assumptions about the nature of friendship that major misconceptions and mis-communications arise.

Given that Chinese culture emphasizes the interdependence of family members and that little or no assistance is available from official organs in the event of difficulties, it is not surprising that for many Chinese the major obligation of friendship is support. True friends are expected to be prepared to offer not only mental or moral support but also a wide range of help and assistance. Such assistance includes the use of influence to help secure access to scarce resources and to find ways around regulations, help in arranging contacts with others who might be similarly useful, and ultimately, financial support where and when needed. The extent to which a person offers assistance of course depends on the degree of friendship, and the ideal of total support (or, as many informants put it, total willingness to sacrifice) is perhaps realized in a comparatively rare number of cases. However, this is the standard by which commitment and friendship tend to be judged. Friendship also involves the giving of moral or mental support and advice in times of difficulties. In Australia, such support would usually be aimed at helping the recipient articulate his or her own desires; in China the aim is often slightly different.

Interactions with friends tend to sound direct, even abrupt, to Australian ears. If interactions with superiors and strangers tend to be more formal than would be the case in Australia, interactions with friends are much more informal. Chinese often comment on the frequency with which Australians apologize to their friends for minor inconveniences—telephoning late at night or asking someone to help in some way, for example. They also notice that Australians tend to use polite forms such as "could you ..." "would you mind ..." even with close friends. In Chinese, more direct forms are usually used between friends. This sometimes results in Chinese appearing to be too direct or demanding when addressing Australians they know well. At the same time, they may interpret Australians as distant and cold in their friendships.

Discussion

Work in groups and discuss the questions.

1. What do you think the rights and obligations of friendship are?

2. Do you agree with the author about the major obligation of Chinese friendship in Paragraph 2? If you do, give more examples.

3. Summarize the opinions in the last paragraph:

Work in pairs. Suppose Speaker A is Chinese and Speaker B is Australian. Explain to each other possible cultural reasons underlying the misconceptions described in this paragraph.

DIRECTNESS

Closely related to the need to "get on with the job without delay" is another widespread American characteristic, namely that of directness. Again commonly used expressions indicate this emphasis:

  call a spade a spade
  don't beat around the bush
  put your cards on the table
  get down to brass tacks
  let the chips fall where they may
  or (more colloquially) "tell it like it is"

It is quite normal for American people to jump right into a subject and say exactly what is on their minds. They often do not couch their comments in carefully gentle phrases to save a person's face. They are not likely to withdraw from a clear cut confrontation between two issues; in fact they often purposefully separate opposing points out from the mainstream of thought to examine and discuss, rather than minimizing them. They are often like metronomes, separating their judgments into two clearly differentiated "beats"; a thing is or *it isn't*; *it is extroverted or introverted*; *black or white*; *developed or underdeveloped*; *good or bad*. Generally speaking, they are not country given to grays, to compromises, to easy melds. They are like a banana—their skin is either on or it is off, whereas much of the world is more like an onion: one skin covers another and another and another, so one can have different depths, different layers; a number of varying truths can all be true at once.

The opposite of "calling a spade a spade" is *indirection*. Many of the world's people do their best to avoid confrontations. They talk around and around a point, making the edges more gentle, leaving easy leeway for retreats or changes of view on either side, showing their sense of respect for the other person by avoiding direct denials or negatives. Rather than saying a shipment **must** go out tomorrow for example, and meeting the reply: "It is **impossible** for it to go out tomorrow—for this and this reason" (confrontation) the same conversation (saving face) might go like this in an "indirect" country:

    Manager: "I certainly hope this shipment can go out no later than tomorrow, for these and these reasons."

    Aide: "I think we may have a few problems; it may be a little bit difficult; but we will try our best."

Both know from that answer that it is unlikely to go out tomorrow. However, the fact is not laid out on line directly; no one will lose face whether it does or does not; the edges are eased. Both will try to "arrange" accordingly; both understand each other clearly.

Those who come from countries which operate in this manner may find business directness hard to accept, until they get used to the pattern and realize that nothing is meant personally. Their personal feelings may be hurt from time to time. Though far more gracious, indirection is a slow approach. Americans look for speed, for facts, for a clear line. Many others look first for grace, for kindness, for dignity and other values. The difference is a matter of priorities.

Discussion

1. With the help of a dictionary work out the meanings of the following expressions individually.

—call a spade a spade

—don't beat around the bush

—put your cards on the table

—get down to brass tacks

—let the chips fall where they may

2. Work in groups. Paraphrase the following expressions.

—jump right into a subject

—couch comments in carefully gentle phrases

—we are not a country given to grays

3. Work in groups. As mentioned in the passage, American conversation style is in directness, i. e. they say what they mean. But for speakers raised in many of the world's cultures, varieties of indirectness are the norm in communication, for example the pattern in China. Discuss the differences in American and Chinese conversation styles and in what way they are like "a banana" or "an onion." Give examples (in your own interactions with foreigners and Chinese).

4. This passage comes from an American author and thus represents an American viewpoint. Considering the influences of culture on conversational styles, people tend to use direct or indirect ways of speaking differently. Sometimes the Westerners' way of speaking is too direct to Chinese ears, sometimes the situation is just the opposite. Try to think of some examples and share them with your group.

Passage 4

Straddling Cultural Divides with Grace

By Marcia Bliss Marks

WHY is it that when you study a foreign language, you never learn the little phrases that let you slip into a culture without all your foreign edges exposed? Every Chinses-language textbook starts out with the standard phrase for greeting people; but as an American, I constantly found myself tongue-tied when it came to seeing guests off at the door. An abrupt goodbye would not do, yet that was all I had ever learned from the awful books. So I would smile and nod, bowing like a Japanese and groping frantically for words that would smooth over the visitors' leaving and make them feel they would be welcome to come again. In my fluster, I often hid behind the skirts of my Chinese husband's graciousness.

Then finally, listening to others, I began to pick up the phrases that eased relations and sent people off with a feeling of mission not only accomplished but surpassed.

Partings for the Chinese involve a certain amount of ritual and a great deal of one-upmanship. Although I'm mot expected to observe or even know all the rules, as a foreigner I've had to learn the expressions of politeness and protest that accompany a leave-taking.

The Chinese feel they must see a guest off to the farthest feasible point-down the flight of stairs to the street below or perhaps all the way to the nearest bus stop. I've sometimes waited half an hour or more for my husband to return from seeing a guest off, since he's gone to the bus stop and waited for the next bus to arrive.

For a less important or perhaps a younger guest, he may simply say, "I won't see you off, all right?" And of course the guest assures him that he would never think of putting him to the trouble of seeing him off. "Don't see me off! Don't see me off!"

That's all very well, but when I'm the guest being seen off, invariably my protests are to no avail, and my hostess or host, or both, insists on seeing me down the stairs and well on my way, with our going through the "Don't bother to see me off" ritual at every landing. If I try to go fast to discourage them from following, they are simply put to the discomfort of having to flee after me. Better to accept the inevitable.

Besides, that's going against Chinese custom, because haste is to be avoided. What do you say when you part from someone? "Go slowly." Not farewell or Godspeed, but "Go slowly." To the Chinese it means "Take care" or "Watch your step" or some such caution, but translated literally it means "Go slow."

That same "slow" is used in another polite expression used by the host at the end of a particularly bountiful and delicious meal to assure his guests what a poor and inadequate host he has been.

American and Chinese cultures are at polar opposites. An American hostess, complimented for her culinary skills, is likely to say, "Oh, I'm so glad you like it. I cooked it especially for you." Not so a Chinese host or hostess (often the husband does the fancy cooking), who will instead apologize profusely for giving you "nothing" even slightly edible and for not showing you enough honor by providing proper dishes.

The same rules hold true with regard to children. American parents speak proudly of their children's accomplishments, telling how Johnny made the school team or Jane made the honor roll. Not so Chinese parents, whose children, even if at the top of their class in school, are always so "naughty," never studying, never listening to their elders, and so forth.

The Chinese take pride in "modesty"; Americans in "straightforwardness." That has left many a Chinese hungry at an American table, for Chinese politeness calls for three refusals before one accepts an offer, and the American hosts take a "no" to mean "no," whether it's the first, second, or third time.

Recently, a member of a delegation sent to China by a large American corporation complained to me about how the Chinese had asked them three times if they would be willing to modify some proposal, and each time the American had said "no" clearly and definitely. My friend was incensed that the Chinese had not taken their word the first time. I recognized the problem immediately and wondered why the Americans had not studied up on cultural differences before coming to China. It would have saved them a lot of perplexity and needless frustration in their negotiations.

Once you've learned the signals and how to respond, life becomes infinitely easier. When guests come, I know I should immediately ask if they'd like a cup of tea. They will respond, "Please don't bother," which is my signal to fetch tea.

Discussion

1. The article discusses some rituals and usual practices of Chinese people in accepting guests and seeing them off. In class discuss the underlying values.

2. Give more examples when Chinese people don't take "no" to mean "no."

3. "American and Chinese cultures are at polar opposites." Individually put in the following table as many differences between Chinese and American cultures as possible, and then compare and

discuss the differences listed in your table with the group members'.

American and Chinese cultures are at polar opposites

Chinese culture	American culture
Apologize for not providing proper dishes	Compliment for culinary skills

Classroom Tasks

Task 1

1. What qualities do you like in a friend? Check the five that you think are the most important.

—sense of humour

—intelligence

—warmth

—physical beauty

—loyalty

—independence (i. e. your friend is not too dependent on you)

—complete honesty

—similar religious beliefs

—similar political beliefs

—similar educational background

—similar likes and dislikes

—helpful

Add other qualities in a friend.

2. Which of the following actions or types of behaviour would probably end a friendship of yours? Circle all that apply.

   a. lending money to a friend
   b. borrowing money from a friend
   c. spending too much time together
   d. one friend becoming involved with someone you didn't like
   e. getting married
   f. having children
   g. getting divorced
   h. changing political views
   i. changing religious views
   j. moving away
   k. one becoming more successful than the other
   l. changing professions

Add other reasons for which friends terminate their relationships.

3. Work in groups. Discuss your choices with your group members.

Task 2

Read the situation individually and then discuss the questions in groups.

1. What do you think might explain the change in some people's attitudes towards John?

2. What advice would you give to both John and his Chinese friend to bridge their misunderstanding?

After having worked in the Australian Embassy in Beijing for some time, John returned to Australia to live. However, although he had many Chinese friends in Australia, he still missed the friends he had made in Beijing. He was therefore delighted when one of his friends wrote to him to tell him that he was coming to study in Australia. John of course told his Chinese friends in Australia about this.

Unfortunately, John's friend failed to get a visa and so was unable to come. Shortly afterwards, John noticed that some of his Chinese friends' attitudes to him had changed. He also heard that some people considered him selfish, cold and even dishonest. John was both puzzled and upset. Why this sudden change? He really couldn't understand it.

Task 3

Read the situation individually and then discuss the questions in groups.

1. What do you think Luz Maria was expecting from Kathy?

2. Suppose you are Luz Maria, what expectation do you have in the situation?

3. Why do you think Kathy made the suggestion? Do you think Kathy intends to be friendly? Try to explain her behaviour based on her possible cultural values.

Luz Maria, a Colombian student, is studying in the United State. Now after two months, her life back home seems far away, except at night when she dreams of her family and friends. She feels sad and lonely. One time Luz Maria spoke with her roommate, Kathy, an American girl about feeling depressed. Kathy suggested that she go to the International Student Counseling office on campus, carefully explaining to her where it was located.

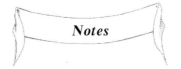

Notes

① Passage 1 is extracted from Levine, D. R. & M. B. Adelman, 1982, *Beyond Language: Intercultural Communication for English as a Second Language*, New Jersey: Prentice-Hall, inc., Englewood Cliffs, pp. 67—69.

Passage 2 is extracted from Brick, J., 1991, *China: A Handbook in Intercultural Communication*, Sydney: Macquarie University, pp. 53—54.

Passage 3 is adapted from Lanier, A. R., 1981, *Living in the U.S.A*, Chicago: Intercultural Press INC, p. 55.

Passage 4 is from *Christian Science Monitor*, 95, 11, 17—23.

Task 1 is from Levine, D. R. & M. B. Adelman, 1982, *Beyond Language: Intercultural Communication for English as a Second Language*, New Jersey: Prentice-Hall, inc., Englewood Cliffs, pp. 82—83.

The passage of Task 2 is taken from Brick, J., 1991, *China: A Handbook in Intercultural Communication*, Sydney: Macquarie University, p. 128.

The passage of Task 3 is based on Archer C. M., 1991, *Living with Strangers in the U.S.A.*, New Jersey: Prentice-Hall, inc, p. 27.

② Irving, K. J., 1986, *Communicating in Context: Intercultural Communication Skills for ESL Students*, New Jersey: World Publishing Corp., p. 146.

跨文化交际意识

　　文化是动态的。每一种文化都处在发展变化中。随着社会的发展,一些新的文化特征随之出现,同时一些旧的特征会消失。譬如:在现代都市生活的人不再需要古老社会需求的基本生存技能,而开车、使用电脑也许是他们生活中的重要技能。文化又是多元的。既是在一种文化内部也存在着多种亚文化,不同行为方式和价值观,存在着看问题的不同角度和对文化现象的不同解释。文化的差异根植于不同的民族心理、不同的价值观。文化没有优劣、好坏之分;不同民族的行为也没有对错之分。本单元旨在启迪学习者在对中西方文化进行对比、讨论时,克服文化心理定势,关注文化的多元性及其发展和变化,以提高跨文化交际的意识。

Unit 11 ①

Intercultural Awareness

No culture is static. Even cultures that have minimal contact with the outside world are affected by changing ecological conditions and events, which in turn change how they experience and understand their own familiar world. ②

Part One Reading and Discussion

Universal Similarities and Particular Differences

One of the most valuable insights that result from interacting with people from many different cultures is the realization that despite particular cultural differences, people all over the world do have a great deal in common. To a large extent fate has determined into what corner of the globe one is born and raised. But once on earth, in a particular cultural environment, there are some choices we do have some control over, and we make those choices according to the patterns of thought and action we have learned in our own cultural environment.

Both culture and communication are very complex. Keeping in mind the mathematical formula that "the whole equals the sum of its parts" may not seem applicable when dealing with people and cultures, but applying such a formula to how we view the world and its cultures might make us more sensitive to the common fate we share with all human beings on this globe. Being aware of the universal aspects of culture that we all share in common, as well as the particular culture difference, can help us function better in any cultural environment.

It is not easy to categorize components of culture that are found in every corner of the world, but the attempt to do so is worthwhile even if the results is neither complete nor perfect. As the list of universals gets longer, one appreciates just how much we all share in common regardless of race, language, or ethnic origin. The three categories of universal culture features that follow (natural environment, man-made environment, and personal and interpersonal environment) are neither complete nor perfect, but they will motivate you to think further about culture, both universal and specific, both yours and somebody else's.

1. Natural Environment
    1) Climate
    2) Geography
    3) Natural Resources
2. Man-Made Environment
    1) food, clothing, and shelter
    2) communications systems:
        a. interpersonal (verbal and non-verbal)
        b. mass communication (entertainment and information)
    3) history
    4) government
    5) artifacts
    6) arts (fine arts, performing arts, literary arts, folk arts)

7) education (formal and informal)
8) religion
9) defense system
10) transportation
11) system for determining rights and wrongs, goods and bads, do's and don'ts
12) system for rewards and punishment
13) system for producing, receiving, and distributing goods and services
14) livelihoods and the division of labor
15) leisure time activities
16) health care systems
17) rites, rituals, and customs
18) attitudes and values about time and space
19) national and local holidays
20) heroes and heroines.

3. Personal and Interpersonal Environment
   1) individual self-perception
   2) interactions with family, friends of same sex, friends of the opposite sex, teachers, colleagues, strangers within one's own culture, people from different cultures, people of different ages, races, ethnic groups, religious groups, economic groups, work groups, and so on.
   3) processes of decision making, problem solving, and role modeling.
   Now that we have looked at the universal aspects across cultures and found similarities, how do we find the differences? One way of discovering cultural differences is to look at the components of the three universal categories and ask questions about them. The answers will reveal the characteristics that identify, explain and distinguish that

particular culture. When the answers from one culture are compared with those from other cultures, differences and similarities will emerge, and there will be a basis for cross-cultural comparison.

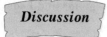

1. Discuss the following views in groups:
—People all over the world do have a great deal in common.
—We make choices according to the patterns of thought and action we have learned in our own cultural environment.
—Being aware of the universal aspects of culture that we all share in common, as well as the particular culture difference, can help us function better in any cultural environment.

2. The passage provides a long list of components of culture. Try to add more to the list.

3. Do some research on one of the universal culture features listed in the passage, and then make a presentation to the class.

For example: The Natural Environment Influences Cultural Values

Stereotypes[3]

Stereotyping is a complex form of categorization that mentally organizes our experiences and guides our behavior toward a particular group of people. Lippmann, who calls attention to this concept as early as 1922, indicated that stereotypes were a means of organizing our images into fixed and simple categories that we use to stand for the entire collection of people. Stereotyping is found in nearly every intercultural situation. The reason for the pervasive nature of stereotypes is that human beings have a psychological need to categorize and classify. The world we confront is too big, too complex, and too transitory for us to know it in all its detail. Hence, we want to classify and pigeonhole. Stereotypes, because they tend to be convenient and expeditious, help us with our classifications. There are a number of reasons that stereotypes, as a form of classification, hamper intercultural communication. First, stereotypes fail to specify individual characteristics. They assume that all members of a group have exactly the same traits. As Atkinson, Morten, and Sue note, "They are rigid preconceptions which are applied to all members of a group or to an individual over a period of time, regardless of individual variations." Second, stereotypes also keep us from being successful as communicators because they are oversimplified, overgeneralized, and/or exaggerated. They are based on half-truths, distortions, and often untrue premises. Therefore, they create inaccurate pictures of the people with whom we are interacting. Third, stereotypes tend to impede intercultural communication in that they repeat and reinforced beliefs until they often become taken for "truth." For years, women were stereotyped as a rather one-dimensional group. The stereotype of women as "homemakers" often keeps women from advancing in the workplace.

　　How do we acquire stereotypes? We are not born with them. Stereotypes, like culture itself, are learned in a variety of ways. First people learn stereotypes from their parents, relatives, and friends. Individuals who hear their parents say "It is too bad that all those Jews are in control of the film industry" are learning stereotypes. Second, stereotypes develop through limited personal contact. If we meet a person from Brazil who is very wealthy, and from this meeting we conclude that all people from Brazil are wealthy, we are acquiring a stereotype from limited data. Finally, many stereotypes are provided by the mass media. Television has been guilty of providing distorted images of many ethnic groups. The problem is that for many people, these false facsimiles often become their private reality.

In most instances, stereotypes are the products of limited, lazy, and misguided perceptions. Their negative effect on intercultural communication is clearly described by Adler:

Stereotypes become counterproductive when we place people in the wrong groups, When we incorrectly describe the group norm, when inappropriately evaluate the group or category, when we confuse the stereotype with the description of a particular individual, and when we fail to modify the stereotype based on our actual observations and experience.

Discussion

Work in groups and discuss the following questions.

According to the author of the passage many stereotypes are provided by the mass media. Find examples in the television or movies of the stereotypes others hole about Chinese culture. In your view, how accurate are they in general? To what extent are the stereotypes correct for you?

Passage 3

Before read the passage, discuss the question in groups: Who would be more willing to take risks, the Chinese or the Americans?

The Dangers of Stereotyping

How often have you heard something like "Well, all Asians

look alike to me! I can't tell one from another."

A lack of awareness and misinformation is the foundation of many cross-cultural conflicts. In order to assist us in better understanding someone from a different cultural background, we often make generalizations and assumptions that classify people by putting them into groupings that are familiar to us. Generalizations can be helpful in the process of learning to understand other cultures. Generalizations can also become dangerous when they result in negative stereotyping—unrealistic and exaggerated characteristics of a group of people.

In a recent paper, Hsee and Weber examine whether American and Chinese respondents could accurately predict the "risk preferences" of their counterparts. The authors chose to compare the two countries for many reasons, including the fact that on issues such as traditional values and current political systems, the U. S. and China stand on almost opposite ends of the continuum and respectively represent Western and Eastern values. Also, both countries currently wield significant impact on the world economy.

Results from the study showed that both the Americans and the Chinese predicted that the Americans would be more willing to take risks. The Americans underestimated the Chinese propensity to seek risk, and the Chinese overestimated the Americans' willingness to take risks. Contrary to these predictions, the authors found that the American participants were considerably more risk-averse than the Chinese. "We are talking about relative terms," says Hsee. "We do not imply that the Americans are not risk-seeking enough or the Chinese are not prudent enough. We do not draw conclusions about what is the optimal level of risk-seeking."

Then why do both the Americans and the Chinese make wrong predictions about the risk preference of their counterparts in the other country? The authors suggest that people often base their predictions on stereotypes. Ubiquitous mass media images which influence our view of cultures tend to promote the stereotype of the risk-seeking, independent American. Popular Chinese stereotypes reflect more cautious, conservative and collectivist characteristics.

The cultural stereotype about Chinese risk aversion may have been correct at some point, suggest Hsee and Weber, but it lags behind current social and economic activities that are reshaping the country and its identity. "China today is very much like America during the Gold Rush period," says Hsee. "The economy is developing rapidly, and many people benefit from taking great risks. This is less true for people in countries with well-developed economies such as U. S. Americans today may not find it beneficial to take unnecessary risks." The authors cite research that highlights changes in the American social and political landscape since the 1960s that may have affected American attitudes toward risk in the direction of less public trust and greater individual caution.

Discussion

1. Is your prediction similar to or different from the result of the study by Hsee and Weber? What is your prediction based on?

2. In intercultural communication have you encountered any stereotypes held by foreigners of Chinese people or culture? Share your examples with your group members.

Passage 4

Culture Change

All cultural knowledge does not perpetually accumulate. At the same time that new cultural traits are added, some old ones are lost because they are no longer useful. For example, most city dwellers today do not have or need the skills required for survival in a wilderness. What is more important in modern urban life are such things as the ability to drive a car, use a computer, and understand how to obtain food in a supermarket or restaurant.

The regular addition and subtraction of cultural traits results in culture change. All cultures change over time. However, the rate of change and the aspects of culture that change vary from society to society. Change can occur as a result of both invention within a society as well as the diffusion of cultural traits from one society to another. Predicting whether a society will adopt new cultural traits or abandon others is complicated by the fact that the various aspects of a culture are closely interwoven into a complex pattern. Changing one trait will have an impact on other traits because they are functionally interconnected. As a result, there commonly is a resistance to major changes. For example, many men in North America and Europe resisted the increase in economic and political opportunities for women over the last century because of the far ranging consequences. It inevitably changed the nature of marriage, the family, and the lives of all men. It also significantly altered the workplace as well as the legal system and the decisions made by governments.

Culture changes, but anthropologists agree that there does

exist in each culture a set of values that endures. These values allow for stability and a certain amount of predictability in our lives.

Discussion

1. In small groups, using examples, discuss the following views:

—Change can occur as a result of both invention and the diffusion of it.

—Predicting whether a society will adopt new cultural traits or abandon others is complicated.

—There commonly is a resistance to major changes.

Classroom Tasks

Task 1

The following passages are taken from an article entitled "Private Life in a Public Culture" by Orville Schell, an American, who lived in Shanghai in 1975. Read them and discuss the questions in groups.

—List the facts which are not true to Chinese present society and give the factual information.

—What do you think caused so many differences between the information in the article and the reality in China today?

—List some value orientations in Chinese culture that are comparatively stable.

For a Chinese, the means of experiencing and expression is the group. He learns in a group, works in a group, lives in a group, and most of the things around him (land, housing, machines, transportation, etc.) are owned by the group.

Neither men nor women in China expend great energy on fashion. (Children dress rather colorfully, but for an adult, to be neat is "correct.") To stand out from the group in the ways fashion engenders is considered to be individualistic and distracting from the great purposes at hand. Although recently there has been more evidence of self-expression in dress, clothes are still, by and large, plain and functional. It is often difficult to tell at first glance if someone is male or female, much less if their physiognomy is comely or not.

Leisure is a word that seems to barely exist in modern Chinese. If the Chinese do not define themselves in terms of being sexual or emotional men and women, they are even less likely to view themselves in terms of "leisure-time identities." The Chinese are not a hedonistic or indulgent people. They do not revel in weekend culture, recreational pilgrimages, gourmet eating, resort life, or even highly individualistic sports. There are no ski weekends. There is no Las Vegas, no Disney World.

Task 2

In one survey carried out in 1980s, visitors from many different countries did not hesitate when asked to list things that were characteristic of life in their own countries. Here are their answers given by Chinese visitors.

Characteristics of my own country
China
There is no privacy.
There is not much divorce.
There are not many private cars or telephones.

Parents/children relations are good.

Listening to the radio is common.

Bicycles are the most common means of transportation.

Suppose, in a new survey, you are asked to list things that were characteristic of life in China today. Make your list and in groups discuss the reasons for the changes.

Task 3

Assume a situation in which you and your identical twin were separated at birth. You were adopted by an American family, and your twin lived in China with your parents. Now you are in your twenties and for the first time you meet each other.

Discuss in class: In what way do you think you are alike and in what way you are different?

Notes

① Passage 1 and Task 2 are extracted from Irving, K. J., 1986, *Communication in Context: Intercultural Communication Skills for ESL Student*, New Jersey: Prentice-Hall, Englewood Cliff, pp. 33—38.

Passage 2 is extracted from Samovor, L. A., R. E. Porter and L. A. Stefani, 2000, *Communication Between Cultures*, Beijing: Foreign Language Teaching and Research Press, pp. 246—247.

Passage 3 is from Millet J. "The Dangers of Stereotyping: A Risky, Offensive and Non-Productive Exercise" located at http://www.culturalsavvy.com;

Passage 4 is extracted from http://www.aucegypt.edu.
② Lustig, M. W. & J. Koester, 2007, *Intercultural Competence: Interpersonal Communication across Cultures*, Shanghai: Shanghai Foreign Language Education Press, p. 333.
③ stereotype: 心理定势。

跨文化交际能力

要在跨文化交际中取得成功必须具有较好的跨文化交际能力,这一能力除包括一般的交际能力外,特别强调在跨文化交际的特殊环境中理解与调和不同文化间可能产生的矛盾的能力。其中较强的跨文化交际意识、愿意参与跨文化交际的态度、对不同文化不同交际规范和风俗习惯的容忍精神以及设身处地考虑问题(移情)的心态,是跨文化交际得以顺利进行和圆满完成的必要保证。跨文化交际能力是可以培养的,只要我们有真诚的意愿和诚恳的态度,通过自己的努力并加上一定的指导,我们就能获得需要的跨文化交际能力,从而在跨文化交往中立于不败之地。本单元收入和编写了一些相关文章及讨论题目,以提高学习者在这方面的意识。

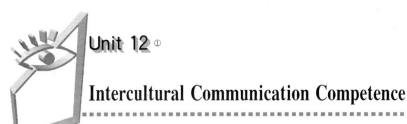

Unit 12 [1]

Intercultural Communication Competence

... we conceive of intercultural communication competence as "the ability to effectively and appropriately execute communication behaviors to elicit a desired response in a specific environment." This definition shows that competent persons must not only know how to interact effectively and appropriately with people and environment, but also know how to fulfill their own communication goals using this ability.

　　　　　　　—Guo-ming Chen, William J. Starosta[2]

Reading and Discussion

The Basics of Intercultural Competence

Eight categories of communication behavior are described in the BASIC (the Behavioral Assessment Scale for Intercultural Competence)[3] instrument, each of which contributes to the achievement of intercultural competence. As each of the categories is described, mentally assess your own ability to communicate. Do you display the behaviors necessary to achieve intercultural competence? From what you now know about intercultural communication, what kinds of changes might make your behavior more appropriate and effective?

Display of Respect	The ability to show respect and positive regard for another person
Orientation to Knowledge	The terms people use to explain themselves and the world around them
Empathy	The capacity to behave as though you understand the world as others do
Interaction Management	Skill in regulating conversations
Task Role Behavior	Behaviors that involve the initiation of ideas related to group problem-solving activities
Relational Role Behavior	Behaviors associated with interpersonal harmony and mediation
Tolerance for Ambiguity	The ability to react to new and ambiguous situations with little visible discomfort
Interaction Posture	The ability to respond to others in descriptive, non-evaluative, and nonjudgmental ways

BASIC dimensions of intercultural competence

Display of Respect Although the need to display respect for others is a culture-general concept, within every culture there are specific ways to show respect and specific expectations about those to whom respect should be shown. What constitutes respect in one culture, then, will not necessarily be so regarded in another culture.

Respect is shown through both verbal and nonverbal symbols. Language that can be interpreted as expressing concern, interest, and an understanding of others will often convey respect, as will formality in language, including the use of titles, the absence of jargon, and an increased attention to politeness rituals. Nonverbal displays of respect include showing attentiveness through the position of the body, facial expressions, and the use of eye contact in prescribed ways. A tone of voice that conveys interest in the other person is another vehicle by which respect is shown. The action of displaying respect increases the likelihood of a judgment of competence.

Orientation to Knowledge④ Orientation to knowledge refers to the terms people use to explain themselves and the world around them. A competent orientation to knowledge occurs when people's actions demonstrate that all experiences and interpretations are individual and personal rather than universally shared by others.

Many actions exhibit people's orientation to knowledge, including the specific words that are used. Among European Americans⑤, for instance, declarative statements that express personal attitudes or opinions as if they were facts, and an absence of qualifiers or modifiers, would show an ineffective orientation to knowledge:

"New Yorkers must be crazy to live in that city."

"Parisians are rude and unfriendly."

In contrast, a competent intercultural communicator acknowledges a personal orientation to knowledge, as illustrated in the following examples:

"I find New York a very difficult place to visit and would not want to live there."

"Many of the people I interacted with when visiting Paris were not friendly or courteous to me."

Empathy Empathy is the ability of individuals to communicate an awareness of another person's thoughts, feelings, and experiences, and such individuals are regarded as more competent in intercultural interactions. Alternatively, those who lack empathy, and who therefore indicate little or no awareness of even the most obvious feelings and thoughts of others, will not be perceived as competent. Empathetic behaviors include verbal statements that identify the experiences of others and nonverbal codes that are complementary to the moods and thoughts of others.

Interaction Management Some individuals are skilled at starting and ending interactions among participants and at taking turns and maintaining a discussion. These interaction management skills are important because through them all participants in an interaction are able to speak and contribute appropriately. In contrast, dominating a conversation or being nonresponsive to the interaction is detrimental to competence. Continuing to engage people in conversation long after they have begun to display signs of disinterest and boredom or ending conversations abruptly may also pose problems. Interaction management skills require knowing how to indicate turn taking both verbally and nonverbally.

Task Role Behavior Because intercultural communication often takes place where individuals are focused on work-related purposes, appropriate task-related role behaviors are very important. Task role behaviors are those that contribute to the group's problem-solving activities—for example, initiating new ideas, requesting further information or facts, seeking clarification of group tasks, evaluating the suggestions of others, and keeping a group on task. The difficulty in this important category is the display of culturally appropriate behaviors. The key is to recognize the strong link to a culture's underlying patterns and to be willing to acknowledge that tasks are accomplished by cultures in multiple ways. Task behaviors are so intimately entwined with cultural expectations about activity and work that it is often difficult to respond appropriately to task expectations that differ from one's own. What one culture defines as a social activity, another may define as a task. For example, socializing at a restaurant or a bar may be seen as a necessary prelude to conducting a business negotiation. Sometimes that socializing is expected to occur over many hours or days, which surprises and dismays many European Americans, who believe that "doing business" is separate from socializing.

Relational Role Behavior   Relational role behaviors concern efforts to build or maintain personal relationships with group members. These behaviors may include verbal and nonverbal messages that demonstrate support for others and that help to solidify feelings of participation. Examples of competent relational role behaviors include harmonizing and mediating conflicts between group members, encouraging participation from others, general displays of interest, and a willingness to compromise one's position for the sake of others.

Tolerance for Ambiguity   Tolerance for ambiguity concerns a person's responses to new, uncertain, and unpredictable intercultural encounters. Some people react to new situations with greater comfort than do others. Some are extremely nervous, highly frustrated, or even hostile toward the new situations and those who may be present in them. Those who do not tolerate ambiguity well may respond to new and unpredictable situations with hostility, anger, shouting, sarcasm, withdrawal, or abruptness.

Others view new situations as a challenge; they seem to do well whenever the unexpected or unpredictable occurs, and they quickly adapt to the demands of changing environments. Competent intercultural communicators are able to cope with the nervousness and frustrations that accompany new or unclear situations, and they are able to adapt quickly to changing demands.

Interaction Posture   Interaction posture refers to the ability to respond to others in a way that is descriptive, nonevaluative, and nonjudgmental. Although the specific verbal and nonverbal messages that express judgments and evaluations can vary from culture to culture, the importance of selecting messages that do not convey evaluative judgments is paramount⑥. Statements based on clear judgments of rights and wrongs indicate a closed or predetermined framework of attitudes, beliefs, and values, and they are used by the evaluative, and less competent, intercultural communicator. Nonevaluative and nonjudgmental actions are characterized by verbal and nonverbal messages based on descriptions rather than on interpretations or evaluations.

Discussion

Work in groups and discuss the following questions.

1. What three BASIC skills would you argue are most important for developing intercultural communication competence?

2. How would you describe your own interaction posture?

3. If you have already had experiences of intercultural communication, recall some of the successful and unsuccessful ones; compare the two kinds of interactions and try to figure out the reasons for the successful ones and the factors for the unsuccessful ones.

Passage 2

Effectively and Appropriately

What criteria should be used to judge ICC⑦ competence? A growing number of communication scholars have embraced Spitzberg's (1988) answer to this question: "Competent communication is interaction that is perceived as effective in fulfilling certain rewarding objectives in a way that is also appropriate to the context in which the interaction occurs"(p. 68). In other words, competent communication consists of behaviors that are regarded as effective and appropriate. Effective communication suggests that people are able to achieve desired personal outcomes. To do so, competent communicators should be able to control and manipulate their social environment to obtain those goals. This presumes that competent communicators are able to identify their goals, assess the resources necessary to obtain those goals, accurately predict the other communicator's responses, choose workable communication strategies, enact those communication strategies, and finally, accurately assess the results of the interaction (Parks, 1976)

Appropriate communication entails the use of messages that are expected in a given context and actions that meet the expectations and demands of the situation. This criterion for communication competence requires the interactant to demonstrate an understanding of the expectations for acceptable behavior in a given situation. Appropriate communicators must recognize the constraints imposed on their behavior by different sets of rules (Lee, 1979), avoid violating those rules with inappropriate (e. g. , impolite, abrasive, or bizarre) responses (Getter & Nowinski, 1981), and enact communication behaviors in an appropriate (e. g. , clear, truthful, considerate, responsive) manner (Allen & Wood, 1978).

The two criteria of effectiveness and appropriateness combine to influence the quality of the interaction. In his recent formulation on ICC competence, Spitzberg (2000) suggested four possible communication styles that may result from the combination of the extremes of the two criteria:

1. Minimizing communication is both inappropriate and ineffective and would obviously be of a low communicative quality.

2. Sufficing⑧ communication is appropriate but ineffective; that is, it is highly accommodating and does nothing objectionable but also accomplishes no personal objectives. Here Spitzberg suggested that the sufficing style is sufficient to meet the basic demands of the context, but it accomplishes nothing more.

3. Maximizing communication occurs when an individual is effective in achieving personal goals but at the cost of being highly inappropriate contextually. This style may include verbal aggression, Machiavellian⑨ behavior, deception, the infringement of others' rights, or the degradation of others.

4. Optimizing communication occurs when interactants simultaneously achieve their personal goals and fulfill the normative expectations of the context.

Although this two-by-two analysis of discrete, binary combinations of the two criteria may a bit simplistic, it helps to provide insight into the dialectics of the competence criteria in social episodes.

Discussion

Work in groups and discuss the following questions.

1. Compare the four communication styles suggested by Spitzberg and think about the advantages of "optimizing communication" as compared with the other three styles. How can you achieve optimizing communication in an intercultural interaction?

2. Read the following intercultural communication event and tell what made it a success:

Unit 12

Alternative communication began early on our Beijing-bound flight. A stout Chinese man in a navy-blue suit was the last to board. He plopped down in the aisle seat to my travel mate, Aaron, and threw his seat belt across his lap.

Neither Aaron nor I had yet learned how to say as much as "hello" in Chinese. We caught the blue-suited man's attention and greeted him with a silent nod and smile.

He turned away with a look of slight disgust, which we interpreted as a message to cease efforts at socialization. We were discouraged by the hostility of this first encounter, but we were determined to improve our pathetic capacity.

We opened our China travel book and started in on the "Useful Phrases" section. As we practiced counting from 1 to 10 quietly, we were started to hear the third resident of our row chime in to correct our pronunciation of the number 2 ("aarrr," not "rrr").

We overeagerly corrected ourselves, thanked him generously, and went on counting, making it clear that constructive criticism was welcome. For the remainder of the flight, Mr. Wang learned over our book and pointed out our mistakes. We shared a few laughs.

It did not matter that much of what Mr. Wang taught us was forgotten or misunderstood. What matters was that his image of us as happily ignorant was dispelled, as was our image of him as hostile. We communicated.

Cultural Awareness

People usually are not aware of their culture. The way that we interact and do things in our everyday lives seems "natural" to us. We are unaware of our culture because we are so close to it and know it so well. For most people, it is as if their learned behavior was biologically inherited. It is usually only when they come into contact with people from another culture that they become aware that their patterns of behavior are not universal.

It is impossible to be entirely objective when we observe another culture. Having been brought up within the context of a particular culture, we have been influenced and shaped by its values, even if we cannot articulate them. Although it should be one's goal to observe another culture with pure objectivity, this is very hard to do. We must remember that in comparing cultures, "different" does not mean "bad" or "inferior" —it just means "different." It is important to remember that although many moments of discomfort occur when we are interacting with people from other cultures, no one culture is inherently better or worse than any other. Each culture has its own set of values, norms, and ways of doing things that are considered "right" for it. That one culture's way of doing things is right for its people does not necessarily mean it is "right" for everybody, and herein lies the potential conflict in cross-cultural encounters.

As a point of reference, an initial step towards developing respect for cultural differences is to look for situations from your own life in which you would behave like a person from another culture. You can learn to appreciate and respect behaviors and values different from your own. Thinking about situations in your own life may help you understand that behaviors that seemingly differ are different only in terms of the type of situation in which you observe them, not in terms of their function. This will prevent you from prematurely valuing a behavior as negative and, more importantly, help you understand what the other person is actually trying to do. Respect is most effectively developed once you realize that most cultural differences are in yourself, even if you have not yet recognized them. For example, you may think that certain ethnic groups are cold and distant. You never know what they are feeling or thinking. But, do you allow yourself to think about why you are warm and hospitable? In fact, the main cultural differences among nations lie in values, not just observable behavior. Once you understand the meaning of others' values, you will have a better grasp of their behavior. Becoming more aware of the influence of cultural values has many positive consequences. It leads to better understanding of ourselves and others. We become more tolerant and less defensive, and we can enjoy cultural differences as well as the similarities.

Discussion

1. Discuss the following views in groups.

—People usually are not aware of their culture until they come into contact with people from another culture.

—In comparing cultures, "different" does not mean "bad" or "inferior."

—That one culture's way of doing things that are considered "right" for its people does not necessary mean it is "right" for everybody.

——Developing respect for cultural differences is to look for situations from your own life in which you would behave like a person from another culture.

——Once you understand the meaning of others' values, you will have a better grasp of their behavior.

2. Make a presentation on the topic "The Connection between Behavior and Values in a Culture" to the class.

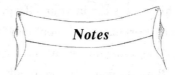

① Passage 1 is extracted from Lustig, M. W. & J. Koester, 2007, *Intercultural Competence: Interpersonal Communication Across Cultures* (5th ed.), Shanghai: Shanghai Foreign Language Education Press, pp. 72—77.

Passage 2 is extracted from Wiseman, R. L., Intercultural Communication Competence, in Gudykunst, W. B. (ed.), 2007, *Cross-cultural and Intercultural communication*, Shang-hai: Shanghai Foreign Language Education Press, pp. 193—194.

The communication episode in the second question for Passage 2 is taken from Lustig, M. W. & J. Koester, 2007, *Intercultural Competence: Interpersonal Communication Across Cultures* (5th ed.), Shanghai: Shanghai Foreign Language Education Press, p. 78.

Passage 3 is extracted from Irving, K. J., 1986, *Communication in Context: Intercultural Communication Skills for ESL Students*, New Jersey: Prentice-Hall, pp. 33—34.

② Chen, Guo-ming & William J. Starosta, 2007, *Foundations of Intercultural Communication*, Shanghai: Shanghai Foreign Language Education Press, pp. 241—242.

③ The BASIC refers to the Behavioral Assessment Scale for Intercultural Competence which was developed by Jolene Koester and Margaret Olebe. It is based on work done originally by Brent Ruben and his colleagues.
④ orientation to knowledge：认识事物的方式。
⑤ European Americans：欧洲裔美国人。
⑥ paramount：最重要的。
⑦ ICC：intercultural communication competence.
⑧ sufficing：刚刚够的。
⑨ Machiavellian：狡猾欺诈的，不择手段的。

部分参考答案

附录给各章节的部分讨论题目提供了一些参考答案。资料均为编著者收集的国内外跨文化交际研究领域的相关资料以及个人积累的资料,以供学习者参考,并希望引发学习者在该领域的更多思考和探讨。

Appendix

Additional Information for Some of the Discussion Questions

Unit 2

Discussion of Passage 2

The development of theories of translation involves a comparison of the responses of original receptors with the responses of those who receive the translated text. In other words, it is important to study the way in which the original receptors of a text interpreted and understood the text, and to compare this with how receptors of the translated text respond to it in terms both of understanding and appreciation. (Jin Di & Nida: 1984, p. 25) Linguistic expressions are often culturally-loaded and can carry cultural information. Failure to receive such information in cross-cultural communication will lead to misunderstanding or even a communication breakdown.

This unit is designed to help learners develop their awareness of the interweave of language and culture.

1. 杯子 cup, glass, mug

疼/痛 ache, sore, pain, hurt

场 the football field, the tennis/badminton/basketball court, the golf course, the skating rink, the hockey arena, the ring (for boxing or wrestling)

a heavy rain 大雨

a heavy responsibility 重大责任

heavy food 油腻/难消化的食物

a heavy heart 沉郁的心情

heavy music 严肃音乐

2. 四合院 compound with rooms around a square courtyard

雍和宫 the Yonghe Temple / the Lama Temple of Peace and Harmony

武术 Gongfu, Chinese martial arts

"三八妇女红旗手" "March 8th Red Banner" / outstanding woman pace setter

3. The New Oxford Dictionary of English defines "individualism" as "the habit or principle of being independent and self-reliant"; the definition given by Longman Dictionary of Contemporary English is "the idea that the rights and freedom of the individual are the most important rights in a society." American culture is said to value individualism. The word "individualism" indicates the commendatory, positive meaning in English, which is different from the Chinese translation "个人主义." Some Chinese scholars suggested that "individualism" can be translated as "个体主义." Compare the meanings of English words "personalism," "egoism" or "selfishness" with the meaning of "个人主义" in Chinese.

In English the word "intellectual" is used to refer to college professors or people who are interested in subjects which need a long period of study. Sometimes the word carries a derogatory meaning. This is quite different from "知识分子" in Chinese, which covers a much wider range of people and it is used in the positive sense.

The English word "peasant" indicates a poor farmer of low social status who owes or rents a small piece of land for cultivation. This is not the meaning referred to by "农民" in Chinese. Compare the meaning of the word "farmer" with "农民."

Each country defines the term "human rights" by what it has. In the United States, human rights refers to the Bill of Rights (e. g. freedom of speech, right to a fair trial). Other countries may define the term differently such as by adequate housing or universal health care.

The word "propaganda" is used chiefly in a derogatory sense meaning information, frequently biased or misleading information, used to promote or publicize a particular political cause or point of view. This is not the same with the meaning of "宣传" in Chinese. Compare the word "publicity" with "宣传."

Compare the meaning of "loyalty" with the connotation of Chinese character "忠" in "忠君" such as "君叫臣死,臣不得不死"; in "忠国" such as "精忠报国"; "filiality" with "孝" in "孝顺父母,敬重长辈" such as "父母在,不远游," "一日为师,终身为父."

Classroom Tasks

Task 2: Language reflects culture. Chinese culture is typical intensive cultivation and is rooted in agriculture. Therefore, many Chinese sayings are connected with land, agriculture or farming activities. English culture, on the contrary, is coastal commerce and there are many sayings closely linked with sea, sailing and fishing activities.

"Religion and culture are inextricably entwined" and is also reflected in language. Therefore, there are many proverbs and sayings connected with Christianity in English and Buddhism in Chinese.

Task 4: Snakes are dangerous animals in both English and Chinese cultures. In ancient Chinese or in Chinese mythology, however, the snake and dragon sometimes are inseparable. Fu Xi and Nü Wa are regarded as the first ancestors of the Chinese nation who are said to have a human-head with a snake body. People who were born in the year of the snake also say that they were born in the year of the young dragon. This associative meaning of the snake is in a positive sense.

A dragon is an evil and strong embodiment in English. It often causes great disasters and guards some mysterious fortunes, as is told in British legends. In Chinese culture, on the contrary, a dragon is a symbol of extreme honor and great power.

Westerners take dogs as their friends and companions, so that in English dogs are used in the commendatory sense in most cases. The connotation of the dog in Chinese is more derogatory, except a few cases indicating the loyalty to its master.

Task 5: In English "white" is in general a festival color, associated things of good omen. "White" is also the color of the clothing generally worn on joyous occasions. Therefore the color term "white" is basically used in a positive sense, symbolizing "happiness," "luck," "justice" and "loyalty." In Chinese, however, the color term "白" is most likely used in a derogative sense, such as death, misfortune, illiteracy, failure, poverty, outside of its role to indicate purity.

The English color term "red" may occasionally refer to "dignity," "happiness," "a great ceremony" such as "red carpet" and "red-letter day," but it is usually used in a derogatory sense associated with "danger" or "violence." In Chinese "红" is in most cases used in a good sense such as getting married, giving birth to a child, congratulating a person on a good beginning in his business. "红" is also associated with "victory," "revolution" in politics.

In English the color term "yellow" is sometimes used in a derogatory sense. On the contrary, the Chinese people, born with yellow skin, having cultivated in the yellow soil, and taking the Yellow River as their place of origin, take pride in their belonging to the yellow race. Xuan Yuan, a legendary ruler of China in remote antiquity was called "黄帝"(Yellow Emperor). "黄" has been the color of emperors and symbolizes imperial power. In modern Chinese, "黄" is also used to refer to pornography in books or magazines.

Unit 3

Discussion of Passage 4

1. Bowing: To greet others, people lower their head slightly.

Forefinger and the middle finger up making a "V" shape: This means "victory." Chinese people often do this when a photograph is being taken of them.

Thumb up and thumb down: If someone shows a thumb straight up to you, that means "Good. Well done." A thumb down means the opposite "Bad."

Laughter/smile: A smile may show affection, convey politeness, or disguise true feeling. Some Western researchers pointed out that the Chinese do not readily show emotion. The reasons for it are rooted in the culture. For the Chinese, displaying too much emotion violates face-saving norms by disrupting harmony and causing conflict. In Chinese culture, a smile, besides showing happiness, can also be used to cover expression of anger or frustration, embarrassment, sorrow, avoidance or even something people do not like to show directly. People from other cultures which do not hide emotions may experience more pressure to understand the Chinese smile.

Silence: Silence can communicate apathy, confusion, repressed hostility, thoughtfulness, contemplation, sadness, regret, obligation, respect, agreement, disagreement, embarrassment, awe, or any number of meanings. Generally, Eastern cultures value silence more than the use of words; in

Western cultures, the opposite is true. To most people in the United States, silence means lack of attention and lack of initiative. A person must speak up to participate. An American saying shows the idea: the squeaky wheel gets the grease. In contrast, the Chinese regard silence as acceptable and customary. Silence (listening) is a sign of politeness, of contemplation or of agreement. This is sometimes misinterpreted by Westerners as "inscrutable."

Silence can mean one is fearful of communicating. This form of silence is associated with the communication as communication apprehension, which refers to an individual's fear or anxiety associated with either real or anticipated communication with another person or persons.

Eye-contact: Western societies commonly agree that eye-contact is important because insufficient or excessive eye contact may create communication barriers. Eye contact serves to show intimacy, attention, and influence. In a conversation too little eye contact may be seen negatively because it conveys lack of interest, inattention, or even mistrust. The expression, "Never trust a person who can't look you in the eye" states the relationship between mistrust and lack of eye contact. In Chinese culture, prolonged eye contact tends to be avoided as a sign of politeness, respect or abeyance, which could easily cause misinterpretation. For example, when delivering a lecture, the Western speaker normally gives direct eye contact to the audience and also expects it in return, which suggests the concentration and interest from the audience.

Classroom Tasks

Task 3: Time—Cultures tend to favor either a past, present, or future orientation with regard to time. Countries such as England and China seem to be past oriented. They value tradition,

Appendix

doing things the way they have always been done. For example, when asked about the monarchy in England, people would say "we have always done it this way." Chinese proverbs such as "Consider the past and you will know the present" and "To forget one's ancestors is to be a brook without a source, a tree without a root" also express the orientation. Americans see themselves as present- and future-oriented. They don't always value the past as deeply as British or Chinese people do. They often value the newest, the most novel and original activity. They run on the "time is money" theory.

Anthropologist Hall proposed that cultures organize time in one of two ways: either monochromic (M-time 时间的单一性) or polychromic (P-time, 时间的多样性). M-time is characteristic of people, who tend to think of time as something fixed in nature, something around them and an ever-present part of the environment. As the word monochromic implies, this approach sees time as lineal, segmented, and manageable. Time is something people must not waste. P-time cultures deal with time holistically. They can interact with more than one person or do more than one thing at a time. For P-time cultures, time is less tangible; hence, feelings of wasted time are not as prevalent as in M-time cultures. Hall pointed out that people of the Western world are on M-time, while people of Asian, African or Latin American cultures are on P-time.

Unit 4

Discussion of Passages 1 and 2

1. Two basic types of families identified by anthropologists are the nuclear family and extended family. Nuclear families are organized around the relationship between husband and wife. The

extended family is based on blood, relations extending over three or more generations.

The nuclear family is adapted in many ways to the requirements of industrial society. Where jobs do not depend on family connections, and where mobility may be required for obtaining employment and career success, a small, flexible unit such as the independent nuclear family has its advantages.

Extended families are clearly adaptive under certain economic and social conditions, and the extended family system prevails in all types of cultivating societies. One advantage of the extended family is that it provides more workers than the nuclear family. This is useful both for food production and for producing and marketing handicrafts, which are generally more important among cultivators. Furthermore, in stable agricultural societies, ownership of land becomes important as a source of pride, prestige, and power. The family becomes attached to the land, knows how to work it, and becomes reluctant to divide it. The extended family is a way of keeping land intact, which provides additional security for individuals in times of crisis. There are also the values of companionship in the extended family, as daily activities are carried out jointly by a number of kin working together. A further advantage is that the extended family provides a sense of participation and dignity for the older person, who lives out his or her last years surrounded by respectful and affectionate kin.

Discussion of Passage 4

6. In individualistic cultures, each individual is the most important part of the social structure. People are concerned with their own personal goals and may not possess great loyalty to groups. In collective cultures, on the other hand, individuals are very loyal to all the groups they are part of, including the work

place, the family, and the community. Within collectivism, people are concerned with the group's ideas and goals, and act in ways that fulfill the group's purposes. Western cultures, in general, fall into the former while Asian the latter. In Western cultures, for example, if people are not happy at their jobs, they are encouraged to look for jobs that will make them happier. People make decisions based on their personal goals and wants. In China, however, the notion of the patriarchal clan system is deeply rooted in the deep structure of its culture. In this culture people are encouraged to be very loyal to their country and their family. People consider the obligation to their groups more than their own individual selves. Children are instructed to feel a lifelong obligation to their parents. When people make choices about marriage, education and work, they always make their decisions together with their families. Their decisions are made based on what their families want them to do and their achievements are mainly for their families.

Classroom Tasks

Task 3: The apparent difference in kinship classification systems between the West and China is the number of terms. The Chinese system distinguishes several kinds of kin that Westerners group together. The Chinese system shows some major principles of Chinese culture and social organization: the values of hierarchy; the importance of the group; the importance of the male principle in inheritance and seniority, etc. Compared to the Chinese system, the Western's simpler and a more flexible system reveals its values of equality, individualism and the nuclear family. For instance, relatives are equally treated no matter if they are from the mother's or the father's side of the family.

Other examples in English terms of address are: In the West mothers- and fathers-in-law are often called by their first names;

children call their uncles and aunts by their first names or Uncle/Aunt + first name.

In China we usually call a person who has a high position by his/her family name plus his/her title like "王科长." In English, however, only a few titles can be used as terms of address, such as King, Queen, President, Doctor, Captain, Professor. The frequent use of one's title in the terms of address in Chinese indicates that people treat those who have more power or high positions more formally and with more respect than other people.

Unit 5

Discussion of Passage 1

1. The chart of the education system in the UK:

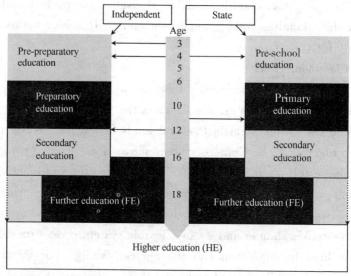

Classroom Tasks

Task 1: In the American preschool one of the rules is "no fighting." American teachers intervene in disputes and fights, primarily by getting children to resolve conflict by verbalizing their

Appendix

feelings. As is seen in Situations 1 and 2 the teacher gave both children a chance to explain what happened and how they felt about the conflict, an approach consistent with the American emphasis on teaching children to express their needs and feelings and the importance of words for social as well as cognitive development.

The teacher did not intervene in an authoritarian fashion, telling a misbehaving child forcefully that that kind of behavior was unacceptable and just could not be tolerated. Instead she made the child think about his behavior and realize his deviance, raising and training children's awareness of their own responsibility for doing things.

Chinese preschool teachers see their main task as controlling children's behavior. One approach is to place importance on modeling children's behavior through verbal comparison and praise. The Chinese teacher emphasizes controlling children before they misbehave, preventing serious deviance by monitoring other's behavior and stepping in before deviance becomes serious. Therefore, the best way to ensure desirable behavior in children is for a teacher to take charge in a classroom, providing order.

Both the traditional Chinese value of Confucianism and Chinese contemporary ideology emphasize that teachers bear an important responsibility in inculcating self-restraint and correct behavior in children.

The many differences in preschool policies and practices in China and the US, in general, are based on fundamentally different cultural values about the nature of children, the importance of the mother-child bond, and the social value of the group in relation to the individual. The Chinese believe that their primary commitment to selflessness and collectivism is best taught outside the family, by the school. The belief of many Americans is that children belong to their parents. American parents also think that getting along in a group is an important aim of preschool, but are much more concerned with intellectual, creative development and happiness of the individual.

Task 2: A learning style is a particular way that an individual receives and processes information. How we learn is influenced by culture. For many Westerners, books may contain facts, opinions and ideas. The facts are open to interpretation, the opinions to dispute and the ideas to discussion. Books are regarded as tools for learning, not the goal of learning. Therefore, critical thinking, judgmental questioning and active initiation of discussion are expected from students in the Western school system. Students are taught to participate actively in the learning process by asking questions and engaging in discussion. Teachers have to impart a body of knowledge, but learners have to discover that knowledge for themselves in order to internalize it. Students should take responsibility for their own learning. They are more likely to enjoy the subject and to succeed at it, if they are involved in the learning process. One aim of teaching is to help learners become independent of teachers, so that learners can use what they learn and continue to learn on their own.

In language teaching it is generally agreed that language is a means of communication. Language is not used in a vacuum but by one person to another in order to communicate a message. Language is not for its own sake, it is used for a purpose—to convey information, emotion or attitude. The most important point for language teaching is directed towards helping achieve this purpose. Therefore, classroom activities should be planned so that they do have a real natural communicative purpose. "Learning by doing" is valued and errors made by learners are seen as a natural part of the learning process. The most important role of the teacher is that of catalyst—they help to make things happen by activating the students. The teacher can play the part of controller, organizer, a resource, tutor providing advice and support to enable students to learn.

In Chinese culture, there is a strong veneration of book learning. The process of education is seen largely as learning a traditional, authoritative body of knowledge. Our education tends to be more theoretical than practical. The teacher exercises greater authority and plays a high directive role in determining and controlling what goes on in the classroom. Students are less likely to challenge or even question the teacher, although this may be changing somewhat with the younger generation. The teacher is expected to be scholar and sage. Some well-known proverbs or sayings about the teacher are as follows: "师者,所以传道授业解惑也" (It takes a teacher to transmit wisdom, impart knowledge and resolve doubts), "教书育人" (impart knowledge and educate people), "师道尊严" (dignity of the teaching profession), "一日为师,终身为父" (A teacher for a day is a father for a lifetime). These examples may help explain some phenomena in the classroom, such as: teachers are addressed with their appropriate titles and last names, or referred to honorably as "teacher." Students rise when the teacher enters the classroom, and say in chorus, "老师好!" Students are expected to erase the blackboard for the teacher, etc.

Unit 6

Discussion of Passage 1

4. Attitudes towards work in some English-speaking countries have been greatly influenced by the "work ethic," which is also called the "Puritan Ethic" or the "Protestant Ethic." This work ethic is a very strong motivator for many people, since work itself

is seen as something "good," having value for both the society and the individual. The ethic was an outcome of the religious belief that material success was a sign of God's favor, and that those who achieved this success were among God's "chosen" and would go to heaven. The work ethic is still important, even though it has lost its religious significance. An outcome of this work value is materialism for Americans: the tendency to be concerned with wealth and possessions.

Chinese culture, developed along the Yellow River basin, is rooted in agriculture. For a long time in the history of China, except in times of war and famine, there was little mobility either socially or geographically. But now mobility is common and especially with the young. Western societies appear to be adaptive where geographical mobility is important. Westerners tend to move from place to place.

Discussion of Passage 3

1. Possible qualities of a future worker:

—developed communication and teamwork skills

—focus on work, not jobs

—to date with technology

—keeping oneself marketable

—always a learner

—ability to develop several potential income sources

Classroom Tasks

Task 1: In general, the interviewer in the West is more likely looking for highly valued traits such as independence, initiative, self-confidence, the ability to work in a team, and the ability to cope in a crisis. A candidate is expected to prove not only his ability to do the job, but also his interest and enthusiasm for the job and the company. If given an opportunity to ask questions at the end of the interview, the applicant usually takes the valuable

Appendix

opportunity to display interest in things like prospects for training, promotion and general upgrading which would demonstrate initiative and readiness to accept a challenge. A curriculum vitae refers not only to a person's academic record, qualifications, but also includes previous experience. The employer's focus is on relevant experience. A job seeker who has spent many years in the same position may be considered to lack independence and initiative. An employee is expected to be loyal to the employer while on the job but is free to change jobs whenever he or she wishes to.

The case is somewhat different in China. In China stability of employment tends to be the norm and to be highly valued. A job seeker who lists a number of job changes is sometimes regarded as unreliable and unstable.

Unit 7

Discussion of Passage 1

2. Asian cultures are steeped in collectivist values. Ranking high among these values are the obligations to show respect for another person, to show humility, to suppress one's individual interests in favor of others, and to avoid offending others. Indirectness and subtlety are the result.

Western cultures, on the other hand, hold to individualist values: candor and directness, the importance of the role of the individual in society, and the rights and freedoms of individuals.

No doubt this sort of East-West dysfunction is abating as global trade and international sophistication grows. People throughout the world are gaining understanding of each other, and international business people are learning (sometimes from their own mistakes) how to get things done.

Discussion of Passage 2

1. In America negotiating is done openly and often forcefully in negotiating sessions. Brief small talk often precedes the business interaction, but the "bottom-line," short-term rewards, and financial arrangements quickly become the focus. It is rarely a rubber-stamp confirmation of a decision already made elsewhere, in private discussions. Compromises are the name of the negotiating game — "I will do this if you will do that." Business cards are exchanged, but generally only when the parties wish to do business in the future. Communication is usually direct, informal, competitive, and at times argumentative.

It is said that because of the impact of social history, business in China is affected by interpersonal connections. In business management, a group relationship is manifested in interpersonal connections ("guanxi"), which overpower the formal organizational structure in many cases. Business contracts are often specified in legal terms but implemented by relying on trust and relationships between the parties involved.

Chinese greetings are formal and use titles and last names. First names are used only among close friends.

Most Americans view gift giving in the business setting as a form of bribery, but for many cultures, gift giving is a standard part of business protocol. Even when visiting a home in the United States, it is not customary to bring a gift, although a small token of flowers, a plant, or a bottle of wine is appreciated. Instead of gifts, letters of thanks are standard in the United States.

Discussion of Passage 3

2. "Goat" in English has a derogative meaning, often associated with rude, foolish.

"White elephant" has the connotation of being troublesome, or a costly but useless item to the owner.

Classroom Tasks

Task 1: In the U. S. "tabling a motion" means not to discuss it, while the same phrase in the Great Britain means to "bring it to the table for discussion."

The British "napkin" means "diaper."

Pronunciation of the word "four" in Japanese sounds like the word "death."

Task 2: What people buy and why is largely influenced by culture. Trademarks usually carry the psychology, emotions, customs and values of the nation. Chinese people like some numbers in particular, such as 6, 8, and 9. Number 6 implies "everything goes well, smoothly," 8 "to make a profit," and 9 "to be forever" following the pronunciation of the Chinese characters respectively.

Therefore, the trademark "三九胃泰" suggests two meanings to Chinese consumers: 1) the main elements of the medicine, which are "三桠苦" and "九里香"; 2) the pronunciation of the characters "九" and "泰" would make the patients have the connotation that taking the medicine will keep them well forever.

"同仁堂" implies that virtue and morality is regarded as more important than business in Chinese tradition, which shows the culture and value of the company. Chinese consumers are sure to trust its products and service.

"STONE," the English translation of the Chinese trademark "四通" implies the following: 1) "firmness" "rock-firm", the literary meaning of the word "stone" in Chinese; 2) insistency, indomitable spirit of the company, the figurative meaning the word suggests in Chinese culture; 3) the company will make a great contribution to the Chinese computer development and be a "stone" to pave its road.

"Nike," an American trademark, is taken from Greek

mythology. It is the goddess of victory and it, therefore, implies the connotative meaning of "Victory" or "Success" to Western consumers. The literary Chinese translation "奈姬" or "娜基" cannot convey the same meaning to Chinese consumers. On the contrary, the present Chinese translation "耐克" can be linked with the Chinese ideas of "being endurable," "can stand wear and tear," and "overcome hardships." To Chinese the connotation of its translation is close to the original one to its native speakers.

Task 3: Other examples of trademarks and their translations might be: Goldlion — 金利来(领带); Sprite — 雪碧(饮料); 雅戈尔—Younger (服装); 新飞—FRESTECH (冰箱 fresh + technology); Toyota—丰田(汽车).

Unit 8

Discussion of Passage 2

American holidays can be divided into four categories based on their content. Holidays for birthdays of famous Americans include the birthdays of George Washington (February 22), Martin Luther King (January 15), and Abraham Lincoln (February 12). Patriotic holidays include Memorial Day (May 30), Veterans Day (November 11), and Independence Day (July 4). Religious holidays include Christmas (December 25) and Easter. Thanksgiving (fourth Thursday in November), Valentine's Day (February 14), St. Patrick's Day (March 17) and Halloween (October 31) have religious origins. Other holidays include New Year's Day (January 1), Mother's Day (the second Sunday in May), Labor Day (the first Monday after September 1), and Columbus Day (October 12).

2. Traditional Chinese Holidays

As with most holidays, there is a story or legend of how that day came to be special. Typically, there are several versions of each story that surround the holiday. When reading about the origin of each holiday, be sure to explore many different versions of the story to see how different people interpret the story.

The Chinese calendar is based on the lunar (moon) cycle. The Lunar New Year is the first new moon after the winter solstice. This means that New Year is not on the same date each year but depends on the movement of the moon. The celebration occurs in January or February.

New Year's Eve

A time of gratitude and family togetherness, New Year's Eve is spent by bidding farewell to the old year and thanking one's ancestors and the gods for their protection. The deafening roar of firecrackers and whistling rockets welcome in the New Year, and frighten away any evil spirits that may be lurking. Chinese people practise many traditions during this time to ensure good luck, health and prosperity in the coming year. At the end of dinner, the children are full of anticipation. The parents and members of the older generations give "hong bao" (red envelope) filled with New Year's money to the children. Finally, to watch the old year out and bring in the New Year, families stay up until the wee hours of New Year's Day

New Year's Day

With the arrival of New Year's Day, life is renewed and the new year begins amidst a din of firecrackers. The Chinese begin the day by worshipping their ancestors. Then the streets become filled with people making New Year's visits to friends and relatives. There is a lively display of dragon dancing, tiger dancing, and other folk activities.

Taboos

To ensure the arrival of luck and wealth in the new year,

several taboos must be heeded. Floors may not be swept and garbage may not be taken out for fear of casting riches out the door. Swearing and quarreling is to be avoided at all costs. And anyone who breaks a dish on this day must quickly say "peace for all time" to avoid misfortune.

More Celebrations

Usually, there is a legend of each day during the celebration. For example, on the second day of the new year, married women return to their family homes. The festive air of celebration continues in this manner until the Lantern Festival, held the fifteenth day of the new year. Then, slowly, life ebbs back to normal.

Lantern Festival

The celebration of the Chinese New Year ends with the Lantern Festival. The festival is known for its beautiful lanterns and dragon dances, special food ("yuan xiao"), and is observed mostly by the rural farmers.

Moon Festival

In the fall of each year, the Chinese celebrate the Moon Festival by grouping together as a family and eating mooncakes.

Dragon Boat Festival

The Dragon Boat Festival also honors a legend, namely that of Qu Yuan, who drowned himself in protest of the corrupt government in ancient China.

Discussion of Passage 3

2. Many children in China are active in sports. Ping-pong, soccer, basketball, and badminton are the most popular types of sports in primary and middle schools. Sports like *Jian Zi*, jumping rope and rubber band skipping are also common. Here are brief descriptions of some of these popular sports.

Ping Pong. Ping-pong is considered to be the national sport of

Appendix

China. Ever since the Chinese team won the world ping-pong championship in the early 1970's, Ping-pong has been a main attraction to the Chinese people. Ping-pong players require much skill and agility. Almost every school provides their students with ping-pong tables either in a corner of the playground or in their gymnasium. The availability of ping-pong tables and its national popularity makes ping-pong a favorite in Chinese schools.

Soccer. During the recent ten years, soccer has received more attention from the Chinese people than ever before. Like the ping-pong tables, soccer fields can be found in almost every school. Students are taught how to play soccer in their PE classes. Some also play soccer after school.

Basketball. Many Chinese students are fond of playing basketball as well. Both boys and girls play basketball in China.

Badminton. Chinese badminton teams have won ten of the world championships in the past twenty years. That is the main reason for Badminton's popularity in China.

Jian Zi, jumping rope and rubber band skipping. have been played by many generations. Many students enjoy playing them because they require great skill and are less space-critical. The rubber band skipping is similar to jump rope, but with large rubber bands. Girls, in particular, use the rubber band to do tricks and sing while they play.

Morning Exercises. Students are often organized by the school leaders to do their morning exercise together in the school's playground or sports ground. In some schools, this is a requirement. It is believed that such refreshing morning exercises are good for the students.

As the Chinese people's living standard keeps improving, more and more people are paying attention to their health. Morning exercises have become a more and more popular way to start the day. Here are some of the types of activities Chinese people do for their morning exercises: Qigong, Tai Ji, Chinese Gong Fu, Martial arts, Sword dances, Morning jogging.

Discussion of Passage 4

2. Unique to China only, Qigong has become an integral part of the Chinese culture. Qigong exercise can produce a myriad of beneficial effects, of which the most common are preventing and curing diseases, strengthening the constitution, avoiding premature aging, and prolonging life. Qigong exercise requires one to relax, to be calm, natural and free from distractions, so that it can remove "stress," and dispel tension. Qigong exercise helps to keep the main and collateral channels in good shape to establish harmony between vital energy and blood, to balance between Yin and Yang, and improve coordination of the nervous system.

Classroom Tasks

Task 2: The concept of the American Dream implies that the United States is a land of boundless opportunity in which upward social and economic mobility and "success" are regularly achieved by the ambitious and hard working, regardless of their social origins. Unfortunately, despite the many individual instances of "rags to riches" stories or even of "self-made" millionaires, the American Dream has been an overly romanticized myth, or perhaps a cruel hoax, for many segments of society including ethnic and racial minorities, women, the poor, and the less talented.

Sport seems an ideal vehicle for understanding the pursuit of the American Dream both because achievement and success are so openly and explicitly emphasized in sport, and because the rags to riches story so often seems to be told by the contemporary mass media with sports figures as the main characters.

Appendix

Unit 9

Discussion of Passage 4

1. *Yin*, which represents the negative, dark, cold, feminine side of all things, and *yang*, which represents the positive, bright, warm, masculine side of all things, must remain in balance and harmony. When they are out of harmony, disease and catastrophe occur. This theory of *yin* and *yang* permeates almost every aspect of the Asian world view, including lifestyle, values, health, and illness. Since everything that is *yin* has a small amount of *yang* in it, and vice versa, Asians tend to view things in shades of gray rather than as absolutes. Sometimes this makes it difficult for Asians to accept a Western diagnosis of a single "cause" of a complaint or to rely on a single form of medical treatment or cure.

Some other treatments in traditional Chinese medicine: Acupuncture, which is also becoming more popular with Westerners, was developed by Chinese physicians in ancient times. Its purpose is to restore the balance between yin and yang. It involves the application of nine needles to specific meridian points. Cupping, suction produced by heating and applying small tubes or hot cups to the forehead or abdomen, produces a negative pressure as they cool, resulting in a circular ecchymosis on the skin. Herbs, in the form of tea, or other drink, are an important part of traditional medicine in all Asian cultures. Herbal remedies require prescriptions from traditional healers.

Classroom Tasks

Task 1: Perhaps the differences in taste are not the cause of the problem. Comparing dietary differences between American and Chinese food from another angle, we may realize that food variety and content is the main difference between them. Chinese food contains many starchy items, such as rice, bean products, and vegetables, while American food has more meat tissue. When eating meals, the human digestive system probably has certain expectations on the quantity of specific items habitually established in the culture. People may feel full when the quota for certain food items has been met but still feel hungry for the unmet ones. For that reason, we may all have problems eating a cross-cultural meal.

Task 2: The typical Chinese table is round or square and the dishes are laid in the centre, which are shared by all. Each participant in the meal is usually equipped with a bowl for *fan* (rice), a pair of chopsticks and a spoon.

Rice is usually doled out from a common pot by the host or hostess. When someone has filled your rice bowl for you, it is accepted with two hands. One places the full bowl in front of oneself and waits until everyone has been served. It is very impolite to begin eating before everyone at the table has had his bowl filled with rice.

In contrast to Western etiquette in which "toothpicks are never used outside the privacy of one's room," toothpicks are provided at most Chinese tables and it is not impolite to give one's teeth a thorough picking at the table, provided one covers one's mouth with the opposite hand.

Task 3: Some examples in the Chinese language which are linked with food are: "民以食为天,""鱼米之乡,""无米之炊,""僧多粥少,""陈谷子烂芝麻,""面有菜色,"etc.

Task 4: Some traditional medical treatments that leave welts difficult to distinguish from the bruises left by beatings have been the source of much misunderstanding between Asian parents and Western educators and social workers who come into contact with their children. These treatments are wrongly interpreted as abuse. Many parents in America whose children have been administered these treatments by family members or healers have been charged with child abuse and have had their children taken from them.

Unit 10

Discussion of Passage 2

3. Summary of the last paragraph

Opinions of Chinese and Australian people about their interaction with friends

Chinese	to	Australian
Chinese interactions with friends	→	direct/abrupt
Chinese interactions with superiors and strangers	→	more formal
too polite/distant/cold	←	Australian interactions with friends

Generally speaking, people from Western cultures do not let personal relations interfere with their professional dealings. For instance, they don't hesitate to chastise a colleague, even if he is a personal friend, for incompetent work. Desire for autonomy or independence in personal relations is important in American culture. While for the Chinese, dependence is desirable because it strengthens relationships between people. Chinese parents, for example take pride in being dependent on their children. Think of Chinese old sayings:在家靠父母,在外靠朋友;多一个朋友多一条路,多一个仇人多一堵墙……

Discussion of Passage 3

4. Examples might be: In China, details about family relationships and roles continue to be "essential information." That may be the reason that questions about age, marital status and children are quite common. Such questions sound direct to foreigners, esp. when meeting them for the first time.

Task 2

The 关系 relationship is popular in China. Some Chinese people assume that this kind of situation is true in Australia. They therefore do not understand that someone who does not use his position to help has an inability to do so.

Task 3

Luz Maria assumes that since she is living with Kathy that they will be friends. When Luz Maria is depressed and talks to Kathy about it, she expects Kathy to listen and discuss her problem. This expectation is based on what friends in Colombia do. In Colombia friends frequently tell one another all their problems and give one another advice. She doesn't know exactly how Americans judge whether people are good friends.

Kathy expects to have a relationship with Luz Maria in which they are roommates only and not share the other areas of their lives. This reveals different cultural values about friendship. She tried to help Luz Maria by suggesting that she see a counselor. In this way she "saved" Luz Maria's face by helping maintain her independence. She was reluctant to get involved; getting involved for Americans means that they are taking away someone's independence. Americans, in order to show care for one another, try to help one another maintain their independence.

Unit 11

Classroom tasks

Task 1

The most powerful elements of culture are those that lie beneath the surface of everyday interaction. These are called *value orientations*. Value orientations are preferences for certain outcomes over others, e. g. private space over public space,

Appendix

deductive thinking over inductive thinking, and so on. These patterns of value orientations tend to be manifested in peoples' behaviors, beliefs, attitudes, and patterns of thinking. All of these are key components in our individual and national identities. Furthermore, it is believed that these powerful, underlying (implicit) elements are the relatively static patterns of value that individuals learn as they grow and develop in their respective social groups. Even though, we may dress similarly to another person, and possibly even speak the same language, the cultural differences "hidden below the surface," may be monumental. These differences may manifest themselves in all sorts of ways such as when one shows up late for a previously scheduled meeting. Thus, each society tends to have its own unique set of value orientations.

Task 3

The twins look just alike, but their mannerism, behavior, attitude, values, and beliefs are vastly different from each other.

Unit 12

Discussion of Passage 2

1. Compared with the other three styles of communication, "optimizing communication" is ideal for intercultural interactions. Because "minimizing communication" and "sufficing communication" are inadequate and would impress others as unwilling or cold; "maximizing communication" goes too far and would frustrate or even offend others. But it is not easy to achieve optimizing communication in an intercultural interaction because the interactants are from different cultures. For example, you may come from a culture which generally appreciates talkativeness, but your conversation partner may be a member of a culture which generally encourages people to be very cautious in talking or

speaking. This would make it hard for you to decide how much and what you should say to the other person or persons in the conversation. Therefore, great care and considerateness are required when you talk to someone from a different culture. To achieve the best result, you would have to strike a balance in between. You should consider both the cultural background of the other or others and his / her or their personal features. This can be done before or / and during the communication. If you can adjust your verbal and nonverbal behaviors appropriately and timely, it is possible at least to reach somewhere near optimizing communication.

2. When their first attempt to communicate with the Chinese man (Mr. Wang) met with the cold shoulder, they felt disappointed but did not give up their efforts. For people of different cultures might have different behaviors when encountering strangers. They did not get frustrated and practiced tolerance. They changed their way of initiating the communication: they made use of the China travel book they had with them and started practicing counting numbers in Chinese, which should be quite appropriate for foreign travelers on a plane bound for China. This drew the Chinese man's attention and quietly aroused his interest and, without knowing, engaged his participation in the interaction. Probably, this indirect strategy of communication did not give the Chinese man, who might be more cautious when faced with strangers, the feeling of intrusion or abruptness, and so is acceptable. As a result, the interaction grew easier and easier for both parties and it turned out to be a success.

References

Brick, J. 1991. *China: A Handbook in Intercultural Communication*. Sydney: Macquarie University.
Deena, R. L. & M. B. Adelman. 1982. *Beyond Language: Intercultural Communication for English as a Second Language*. New Jersey: Prentice-Hall, Inc., Englewood Cliffs.
Guo Xiaomin. 1999. *On Fixed Expressions about Animals and Their Translation*. Unpublished thesis.
Harvey, P. & R. Jones. 1992. *Britain Explored*. London: Longman.
Huang Shu-min. 1996. "A Cross-Cultural Experience: A Chinese Anthropologist in the United States." In Angeloni, E. (ed.) *Annual Editions: Anthropology 96/97*. Guilford: Dushkin Publishing Group/Brown & Benchmark Publishers.
Irving, K. J. 1986. *Communicating in Context—Intercultural Communication Skills for ESL Students*. New Jersey: Prentice-Hall.
Jands, F. E. 1995. *Intercultural Communication: An Introduction*. California: Sage Publications Ltd.
Jensen, J. V. "Perspective on Nonverbal Intercultural Communication." In 胡文仲 (ed.) 1990. *Selected Readings in Intercultural Communication*. 湖南教育出版社.
Jin Di and E. A. Nida. 1984. *On Translation: With Special*

Reference to Chinese and English. 北京：中国对外翻译出版公司.

Lanier, A. R. 1981. *Living in the U.S.A.* Chicago：Intercultural Press Inc.

Liu Xiaohui. 1999. *On Cultural Connotations of Basic Color Terms and Their Translation*. Unpublished thesis.

Markstein, L. & L. Hirasawa. 1977. *Expanding Reading Skills*. Rowley：Newbury House Publishers, Inc.

Matikainen, T. & C. B. Duffy. 2000. "Developing Cultural Understanding." In *Forum*. 38 (3).

Nanda, S. and R. L. Warms. 1998. *Cultural Anthropology*. 6th ed. Washington：Wadsworth Publishing Company.

Samovar, L. A. et al. 2000. *Communication Between Cultures*. Beijing：Foreign Language Teaching and Research Press.

Tregidgo, P. S. 1978. *A Background to English*. Hong Kong：Longman.

董广杰，2001，《龙的传人与龙的精神——中国传统文化透视》。中国纺织出版社.

彭石玉，2001，"汉字商标词的跨文化传统"，《外语与外语教学》。2001年第4期.

浦小君，1991，"外语教学与跨文化交际技能"，《外语界》。1991年第2期.

王逢鑫，1997，"中国品牌命名的文化含义"，《语文研究群言集》。广州：中山大学出版社.

谢建平，2001，"试论民族心理与商标语言创意"，《外语与外语教学》。2001年第12期.

张岱年、方克立，1994，《中国文化概论》。北京：北京师范大学出版社.

http://www.postgradmed.com
http://www.multicultural.vt.edu
http://www.britishcouncil.org

References

http://www.hrzone.com

http://web.fccj.org

http://www.saf.ukplatt.edu

http://fletcher.tufts.edu

http://www.jiad.org

http://www.crossculture.com

http://www.mnc.ab.ca

http://www.culturalsavvy.com

http://usinfo.state.gov

http://www.makingconnections.state.mn.us

普通高等教育"十一五"国家级规划教材

北京高等教育精品教材
BEIJING GAODENG JIAOYU JINGPIN JIAOCAI

新编英语专业口语教程系列　　**总主编：齐乃政**

【教材特点】　本教材的编写原则：以《普通高等学校英语专业教学大纲》为依据；以交际话题的难易为依据——具体至抽象，由浅入深；以功能意念为线索，融功能意念于交际之中；以日常生活中经常使用的话题为重点。

本教材在编写中努力体现：听说结合；口语教材新颖实用；练习形式多样；难度阶梯化。

新编英语专业口语教程(1)	齐乃政	16开	定价：18.00	978-7-301-06897-2/H·0974
新编英语专业口语教程(2)	齐乃政	16开	定价：28.00	978-7-301-08376-9/H·1376
新编英语专业口语教程(3)	齐乃政	16开	定价：28.00	978-7-301-05713-X/H·0761
新编英语专业口语教程(4)	齐乃政	16开	定价：30.00	978-7-301-08489-7/H·1391